HOW TO ADD
FLAVOR

HOW TO ADD FLAVOR

AN INTRODUCTION TO SPICES & HERBS

Ian Hemphill & Kate McIntosh

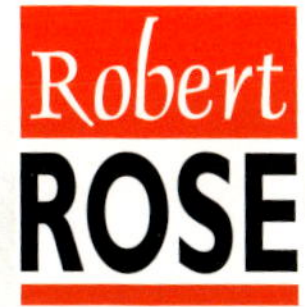

How to Add Flavor

For complete cataloguing information, see page 160.

Disclaimer

Editor: Amy Treadwell
Copyeditor: Wendy Potter
Proofreader: Kelly Jones
Indexer: Gillian Watts
Design and Production: PageWave Graphics Inc.
Photography: Natercia Cabeceiras
Food Styling: Sonia Lizotte

Published by Robert Rose Inc.
120 Eglinton Avenue East, Suite 800, Toronto, Ontario, Canada M4P 1E2
Tel: (416) 322-6552 Fax: (416) 322-6936
www.robertrose.ca

Printed and bound in China

1 2 3 4 5 6 7 8 9 ESP 33 32 31 30 29 28 27 26 25

To my wife and
Kate's mother,
Elizabeth Hemphill.

Contents

Introduction

As a child, you tend to take your environment for granted, not appreciating how much you absorb by osmosis. Our family home was often strewn with drying herbs. I'd earn pocket money helping Dad harvest herbs to be laid out on drying racks.

After WWII, refugees from various parts of the world brought a new repertoire of flavors and cooking styles to the countries that welcomed them, meals dependent on the creative use of herbs and spices that these cultures had enjoyed for centuries.

My mother was a home cook, so I recall coming home from school to an aromatic kitchen filled with cooking smells from her daily recipe testing. This was when it became obvious to me that creating tasty food was an art, not a science.

In the late 1960s, I was inordinately fortunate to meet the love of my life, Liz, whom I married in 1970. While working out how to support a family, I helped Dad in the family business, which involved packing spices into thousands of jars, making spice mixes and packing cartons of spices to be shipped all over Australia. I found I was enjoying the diverse experiences of the herb and spice business more than I expected, especially a task that remains one of my favorites to this day: holding spice appreciation classes and presenting lectures on spices.

Liz worked in the family business when she could find the time while raising our daughters. She also wrote a book in the mid-1970s called *Your First Book of Herb Gardening*.

Our girls have many fond memories of playing in their grandparents' herb garden. So much so that Kate, our eldest daughter, not only graduated as a chef from a renowned food school in London, but is also the creator of the recipes in this book.

When my parents retired, I continued to work in the spice industry, which took me to managing a spice company in Singapore, attending spice conferences in India, consulting on herbs and spices for food businesses and operating as a spice broker for a Danish spice company. In 1997, Liz and I started our own family business called Herbie's Spices, an artisanal specialty spice company in Australia.

This brings Kate and me, with tireless assistance from Liz, to creating *How to Add Flavor: An Introduction to Spices & Herbs*.

Let's Begin

IT'S AN UNDISPUTED FACT that everyone must eat to stay alive. Even the most boring food can keep you alive — but who wants to live on bland food, when it's so easy to make it tasty and interesting?

People often say they can't cook with spices even when they have been proficient in the kitchen for many years. It seems there is uncertainty surrounding the act of adding spice to food, so we're here to reassure you just how wonderful and easy it is to add great flavors to your everyday cooking.

Whenever I cook something, even the simplest barbecue, I'm told, "Wow, you are such a great cook."

The reason people say this is because the food tastes amazing simply due to the use of herbs and spices to deliver wonderful flavors. You can get the same results by browsing the information we are sharing with you, including the easy ways to add readily available ingredients to basic proteins and vegetables and the section with 60 recipes using the spice and herbs. Try our tips and recipes out yourself, and then enjoy sharing your spice experiences with family and friends and bask in the compliments!

THE SPICE TRADE

Spices, being dried, could be easily transported over long distances, as was done for centuries along various trade routes and silk roads by camel trains, and subsequently by sea. Thus, a lucrative spice trade developed, incentivizing explorers to take huge risks in the hope of finding a source of supply that could be monopolized and traded at a huge profit.

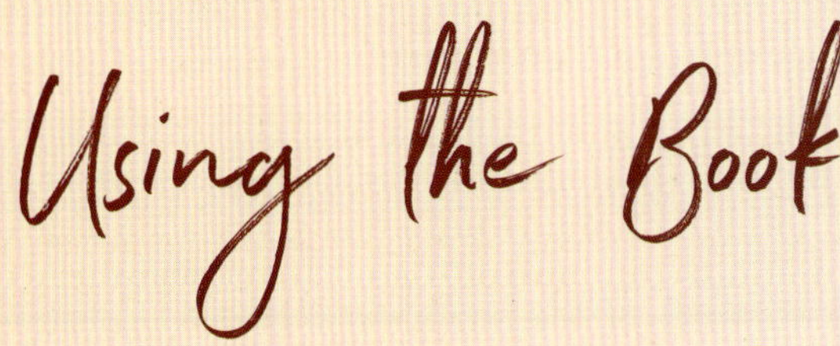

We've organized this book into three basic sections and we encourage you to read through them before starting to cook.

First, there are profiles of what we have found are the fifteen most popular spices and herbs used in cooking today. We've given you an overview of each one, including helpful information on the aromas and flavors and what foods pair best with them.

Next is the Spice and Herb Recipe Tutorial, which contains four basic recipes — Skillet Chicken Breast with Pan Sauce, Classic Pot Roast, Salmon Parcels and Crispy Fried Tofu. Not only are these designed to teach you how to cook simple proteins, but when you choose one of the four Flavor Change-Ups that go with each recipe, you will begin to learn how using different spices and herbs can change the flavor profile and turn a perfectly nice dish into something spectacular.

Finally, you can take your newfound skills to the next level by trying one of our 60 exciting, easy-to-make recipes, using all the spices and herbs you just learned about.

Spices and Herbs Defined

We all talk about herbs and spices constantly, but rarely think of what the difference between the two categories is or how this influences the way we use them. So, let's go over some basics.

An herb is what we define as the leafy part of a plant used in cooking, like basil, mint and rosemary.

A spice may come from any other part of the plant, such as the bark, berries, roots, fruits or seeds. Examples include cinnamon, peppercorns, turmeric, chiles and cumin.

We can use herbs in fresh or dried form, depending on the recipe and, to some degree, what is available at the time. Spices are mostly used in dried form, as it is the drying process that creates their distinct flavors.

FROM THE EARLIEST TIMES . . .

The first fragmented records of the use of spices date as far back as 2600 BCE. Egyptians at that time knew about and appreciated the medicinal properties of onions and garlic, so these foods were fed to the 100,000 laborers who worked on the construction of the Great Pyramid of Cheops in Egypt.

In another example, a long list of aromatic plants, including thyme, sesame, cardamom, turmeric, saffron, poppy, garlic, cumin, anise and coriander, was discovered in a scroll of cuneiform script, one of the oldest forms of known writing. It was in the great library in Nineveh (in modern-day Iraq), established by King Ashurbanipal of Assyria (668–627 BCE).

Buying and Storage

All the herbs and spices in this book are readily available in stores; however, there are some important things to remember when shopping for, storing and preparing them.

For fresh herbs, look for unwilted leaves that don't have any noticeable brown or black spots on them, which is a sign of being past their best. When you get your herbs home, sit the bunch in a glass with the bottom of their stems in clean water, shroud with a light plastic bag and store in the refrigerator. When picking the leaves from the stems, always strip them off in an upward motion. A downward motion will take some of the firmer stem along with the leaf, which isn't so desirable in your food.

For dried herbs and spices, it is always best to buy them packed in resealable, airtight pouches or to place them in jars. Store at home away from heat, light and humidity, as these factors will shorten the shelf life. Properly processed dried herbs and spices will never go bad; they will just lose their pungency over time. When using these, never put a wet spoon in the container or hold the container over a steaming saucepan, as this introduces moisture, which will shorten the time the herb or spice is at its best. On average, whole spices will keep their flavor for three or more years, and dried herbs and powdered spices will stay tasty for around eighteen months.

STORAGE TIP

Be careful when storing spices in the fridge or freezer. When you take the package out, condensation will form, introducing moisture. If you must store them that way, make sure all signs of condensation have disappeared before you open the package.

Using Whole or Ground

Sometimes recipes will use whole spices and sometimes ground. This is because the way they deliver the taste and appearance in a recipe will be different.

For example, whole spices such as cinnamon and cumin will be used to flavor rice while it is cooking, but don't change the rice's color the way cinnamon powder or ground cumin would.

Ground spices and rubbed herbs are needed when you want a rub to use on meats before cooking. These will also release their flavors quickly, as grinding releases the oils that give them their personality. In a Moroccan tagine, ground spices help to form the delicious gravy.

Growing Your Own

Herb plants, available from nurseries and plant stores, are not difficult to grow if you have space in the garden or a place to keep them in pots or a window box. Talk to the folks at the nursery, who can provide a wealth of information to start you on your herb-growing journey.

Herbs are classified as either annual or perennial. Annuals like cilantro only grow for one year (some maybe two), while perennials like rosemary will grow for many years.

The few basic requirements are well-drained soil or potting mix, sunshine and fresh air. This means herbs will not thrive indoors unless you have a window box where they can be caressed by the wonders of a natural environment.

Your annuals will flower every year. After flowering, the herb goes to seed and its root system dies. To prolong growth, get more leaves sprouting and encourage the herb to live for longer, nip off flower buds as soon as they appear, to interrupt the life cycle.

KOSHER AND HALAL

You will notice that many herbs and spices and some spice blends will have on the label that they are kosher or halal, or both. This is because, under the dietary guidelines that come from their respective religious texts, there are rules with respect to how some foods are prepared, most notably regarding meat. Other foods are restricted from the diet. This means that an herb, a spice or a spice blend labeled this way won't contain an ingredient that is not allowed.

HEALTHY EATING

All spices are high in micronutrients, antioxidants and phytochemicals, making them a beneficial addition to your diet. The majority are low in fat and sodium and contain vitamins associated with good health. Many references to the potential health benefits of an herb or a spice might commence with statements like "May help prevent inflammation . . ." However, please be aware that all the compounds in herbs and spices will benefit most individuals, while not necessarily alleviating a particular disease. Most importantly, using herbs and spices in your meals reduces the need for foods that are high in artificial flavor enhancers, fats, sugars and salt. Natural, wholesome food that tastes great is your best insurance against illness and disease.

These two important flavor enhancers in your repertoire have traditionally gone hand in hand. "Pass the salt and pepper, please" is a common conversation starter at the table.

Recipes will often state "season to taste," but we know some people wonder, *season with what?*

This phrase in recipes always means to add salt to suit your personal preference. Some confusion has arisen among home cooks because many spice blends are called seasonings. So, in this book, when we say to season, we will always state with what.

Salt

Although it is not a spice, salt was undoubtedly the first known seasoning, with a history that dates to the dawn of humanity.

Salt is one of the fundamental tastes, along with sweet, sour, bitter and umami. The component responsible for the salty taste is sodium chloride ($NaCl$). Various other minerals, such as salts of iron or other naturally occurring substances, contribute to the flavor characteristics of salts from different parts of the world.

When it comes to determining the right amount of salt, it should be added toward the end of cooking, because any reduction taking place during cooking time will concentrate the salt content in ratio to the volume of ingredients in the dish being prepared.

Salt enhances the flavor of food by reacting with our taste receptors and masking perceptions of bitterness, as well as increasing the tastes of sweet, sour and umami. Salt is also an important element in the preservation process due to its ability to draw out moisture and inhibit microbial activity.

In recent years, special types of sea salt have become popular for their flavor attributes and the texture variations most noticeable when these salts are sprinkled over food after it has been cooked. Each type is distinguished by its origins.

Table salt is the standard, fine-grained salt that is most commonly found in salt shakers, adding saltiness with no other tastes or textures.

Kosher salt is a common salt that has nothing added to it, such as free-flowing additives or iodine. This seasoning is used for "koshering" meats, a process that draws blood from meat before it is cooked.

For more salt varieties, see the next page.

PAIRINGS

Salt pairs with all savory foods and is also added in small amounts to food items as varied as chocolate confections, pancake batter, cakes and breads.

HEALTH

In all its history, it seems that salt has never suffered such criticism as has been leveled at it in recent years as a cause of high blood pressure and other ailments. It has been well documented how the excessive use of nature's humblest taste enhancer can lead to health problems. Perhaps this was because of its abuse.

Nonetheless, salt remains one of the five fundamental tastes; without it – in balance – our diets would indeed be bland. Healthy adults need only about two to five grams of salt a day, an amount largely provided by the food we eat.

Pepper

The pepper we are referring to here is the peppercorn, a berry that is harvested from *Piper nigrum*, a tropical climbing vine native to the south of India and grown in many tropical countries. This pepper is not to be confused with chile peppers. There are three kinds of peppercorn produced by the *Piper nigrum* vine: black, white and green. There is also pink peppercorn, which comes from a different plant.

When a global market is as large as that for black pepper, 150,000 tons to 200,000 tons a year, there will be a plethora of qualities and grades available.

Avoid peppercorns that look at all moldy, as they should always be dark brown or black with a matte finish rather than a shiny appearance.

Black pepper has been the most traded spice in the world for many centuries, and the history of pepper—acknowledged as the *King of Spices*—is a major part of the history of the spice trade itself.

PAIRINGS

Besides always being alongside its stablemate salt, pepper can pair with any other spice to add its pleasing fragrance and flavor, along with its pleasantly stimulating bite. It can also be paired with certain foods for an impactful meal or snack. As surprising as it may sound, a light sprinkling of black pepper over fresh strawberries is delicious.

HEALTH

Black pepper is high in antioxidants and phytochemicals. The peppercorn contains a natural alkaloid called piperine, which gives both black and white pepper their spicy heat. This alkaloid is also important in making the curcumin in turmeric more bioactive in anti-inflammatory tablets. Even though the amount of piperine consumed in pepper is quite small, its ability to reduce free radicals may help in the recovery from inflammatory diseases such as heart disease.

For more peppercorn varieties, see the next page.

Fleur de sel is an expensive, almost sweet, floral-tasting salt that has been harvested from natural salt pan areas within the Brittany region of France.

Celtic sea salt, or gray salt as it is sometimes called, comes from the same vicinity. It is hand-raked and has a coarse look and moist texture.

Maldon sea salt is from Maldon in Essex, England. Its characteristic flaky texture is achieved by spreading the concentrated sea water solution, after initial evaporation, over flat surfaces where it dries out, leaving flaky crystals, before being scraped up.

Himalayan pink salt is a mined salt from Pakistan's Punjab region. It gets its pink color and unique flavor from a variety of minerals contained in the large crystals.

Black Hawaiian salt is mined around Hawaii's islands. It's blended with activated charcoal and other ingredients to give it the black color and slightly smoky flavor.

Iodized salt was developed because it was noted that millions of people in the world were suffering from an iodine deficiency. It is a mixture of table salt and inorganic compounds of iodine and tastes no different to table salt.

Seasoned salts and spiced salts are something you can make yourself. They are mostly salt, which costs very little, with a spice or spice blend added.

Herb and vegetable salts are formulated using plants or extracts of plants and seaweed with high levels of mineral salts occurring within them naturally. Most of these salts may contain substantial amounts of common salt.

Black pepper is the most common type of peppercorn, produced by harvesting unripe berries and putting them out in the sun for about a week to dry. Drying activates an enzyme in the skin of the peppercorn, turning it black and creating a volatile oil, which gives black pepper its characteristic rich, oily aroma and full-bodied flavor.

White pepper is made by harvesting ripe peppercorns and soaking them in water for several days, after which time they are taken out and rubbed to remove the outer skin. White pepper is a good way to introduce heat to a white sauce without also adding black specks. In addition, it offers a sharper, hotter flavor profile.

Green peppercorns can be purchased in jars in salty brine, which stops the enzyme from turning them black. These are also available dried. The flavor of green peppercorns is milder than black pepper.

Pink peppercorns are not actually included in our recipes. Ripe pink peppercorns are hard to find and can be purchased only in brine. However, you can sometimes find dried pink peppercorns at the grocery store, but they are not a true pepper. Instead, they are a berry from a Brazilian tree with a juniper-like flavor. Feel free to try them, but don't put either of these in a pepper mill, as they will clog the mechanism.

The Spice & Herb Pantry

Chile
Coriander
Cinnamon
Garlic
Ginger
Mint
Rosemary
Thyme
Turmeric

Allspice

Allspice is actually a berry harvested from a tropical evergreen tree native to Jamaica and other Caribbean islands. Christopher Columbus's journal of 1492 mentions that when the people of Cuba were shown black peppercorns, it led them to communicating that there was an abundance of these in the area. So, word got back to Spain that this was "pepper," and for many years, it was called Jamaica pepper.

Even King Philip IV of Spain, on thinking that pepper grew wild in Jamaica, sent minions to get some "la pimienta de Jamaica" to boost the royal coffers. Imagine the disappointment when they returned with, what was at that time, almost worthless allspice! Confusion reigned for some time, until the term "allspice" was universally adopted as the spice's common name, because its flavor was reminiscent of a mixture of cloves, cinnamon and nutmeg.

PLANTATION WALKS
Allspice plantations in Jamaica are called "walks," as the trees grow in rows along fence lines. The walks came into being when birds, who ate the green berries, perched on fence lines and expelled seeds in their droppings. Presto! Allspice trees grew along these fence lines.

Aroma

As is so often the case with spices, the magic that creates their scent (and flavors) comes to the fore through a completely natural drying process, which turns the green, unripe berries into a much-loved, useful ingredient. Just like cloves, pepper and vanilla, drying this spice in the sun activates naturally occurring enzymes that turns them dark brown and creates eugenol, the volatile oil that gives allspice its characteristic fragrance, which is much like mild cloves and, surprisingly, fresh basil leaves!

Flavor

The same volatile oil that gives allspice its aroma also helps deliver, along with other compounds, a distinct clove-like flavor that has a touch of sun-dried fruitiness. It's amazing to know that eugenol can also be found in cloves, cinnamon, bay leaves and star anise.

Pairings

Allspice is an excellent substitute for cloves, but is milder and fruitier, lacking that strong medicinal reminder of the dentist! Ground allspice is a key ingredient in Jamaican jerk seasoning and is used in curry powders, tagines, Chinese dishes and tomato and barbecue sauces. The whole berries are used in pickling spices.

You don't need to use much. We use it in recipes to add depth of flavor and, like basil, it goes well in tomato-based Italian recipes.

Ground allspice can be found at supermarkets, should be dark brown; not pale, grainy or dusty. Store it as you would all your ground spices, in airtight packaging.

Basil

Basil is one of the most popular herbs. There are many varieties, though sweet basil is the most readily available at grocery stores. Sweet basil can grow into small shrubs, with deep green, oval leaves attached to grooved and square stems.

Fresh basil is generally sold in bunches, providing plenty of tender, delicious leaves for most recipes. Avoid buying fresh basil that is wilted or has black marks on the leaves; it's not as fresh as it should be.

As a seasonal, sun-loving plant, fresh basil is most abundant in stores and economically priced during the summer months.

Aroma

As a little boy in my mother's herb garden, basil was the first herb I could identify by aroma. For me, basil's refreshing, clove-anise-like aroma conjures up memories of summer. This is hardly surprising when one considers how this warmth-loving herb thrives in heat and expires at the first chill of winter.

Flavor

Fresh basil's flavor is bright, clean and clove-like with deep warmth that seems to complement every food to which it is added. It is interesting to notice that, although the fresh leaves seem quite pungent, the actual flavor the herb imparts is never overpowering, a phenomenon that seems to be unique to basil. This means that it is almost impossible to use too much fresh basil in a salad, pesto (which is mostly fresh basil) and tomato-based recipes.

When fresh basil is out of season, dried basil may be used as a substitute in some recipes. The moisture content is lower and the fresh aroma is lost, so the flavor becomes concentrated and stronger. Dried basil is best suited to recipes that are being cooked, but not so suitable for recipes calling for fresh basil, like salads or pesto.

Pairings

Basil's unique culinary profile pairs exceptionally well with tomato and tomato-based dishes. In fact, gardeners will tell you basil and tomatoes are companion plants.

Fresh basil is used in Italian and southern European cuisines, possibly because it is abundant in these warmer climates. The herb complements almost every food, from eggplant, zucchini, and squash, to lentils and new potatoes. Try basil blended into cream cheese for a sandwich. The herb's clean, fresh notes enhance chicken, pork, fish and shellfish.

Dried basil is best in cooked tomato dishes, including Bolognese and other pasta sauces, and baked, barbecued, roasted or fried chicken. To use fresh basil in these recipes, be sure to add it in the last 15 minutes of cooking to retain its fresh flavor notes.

Storage

Basil will keep in the refrigerator for a week or more. Wrap paper towel around the stems, wet it and seal it all in a plastic bag.

Chile

Known as red pepper and cayenne pepper, chile plants bear fruits of varying sizes and colors, each with different levels of heat. The heat comes from capsaicin, which is found mostly in the seeds and the seed-bearing placenta in the chile, but it's also in the skin. Wear gloves if possible and do not touch your face or eyes when cutting chiles.

There are too many chile varieties to mention here, so we've focused on the most readily available and easiest to use: the fresh green, yellow and red pods, along with hot pepper flakes, ground chile, red pepper and cayenne pepper.

The heat level of chiles used in these recipes can be described as medium. We use cayenne pepper, which is a hot, ground chile for more heat.

Be aware: chili powder sold in stores is generally a spice blend that contains cumin, paprika, garlic and other ingredients as well as ground chile. Don't buy it—we'll show you how to mix the right spices together when these flavors are required.

Aroma

Fresh chiles have a clean, light, bell pepper-style aroma that does not indicate how hot the chile is.

When a chile is dried, you get some caramelization of the sugars in the pods that have developed on ripening. These sugars and the volatile oils and compounds create a deeper, more robust aroma, which will vary depending on the variety. For example, ground ancho chile will have a different aroma than ground Kashmiri chile.

Flavor

The flavor is like bell peppers and sweet paprika. Dried chiles have deep, robust flavor notes. Think of the difference between a fresh tomato and a sun-dried tomato and you get the idea.

Use fresh chiles in dishes that are not cooked (salads) or are briefly cooked (stir-fries, omelets and Asian soups). Dried chiles are used with longer cooking times (curries, tagines and casseroles) and with stronger flavors (pizzas, pasta sauces, Mexican recipes). It all depends on your taste preferences.

Pairings

The agreeable fruity flavors and characteristic spicy heat of chiles have made them one of the most traded and popular of all spices.

Cuisines that feature a lot of chiles are Mexican and Asian, and can be found in curries from all cultures, especially Indian, Moroccan and Middle Eastern. If you love the taste and a little bite, they go with almost anything.

Storage

When buying fresh chiles, make sure the pepper's skin is not wrinkled, which is an indication that they are not fresh.

Store fresh chiles in a bowl at room temperature for a few days until needed, or for longer in the refrigerator, where they will keep for 2 to 3 weeks. Dried whole chiles and the ground and flaked forms are stored in airtight packaging.

Cilantro/Coriander

Here we have an herb and a spice that come from the same plant. Cilantro is the term for the leaves, an herb that is nearly always used fresh. The seed, collected and dried from the plant after flowering, is a spice called coriander.

The plant is a vigorous annual that gives us leaves, stems and roots that bear the same distinctive aroma and flavor. The leaves are dark green and resemble the shape of Italian parsley leaves, hence the other common name: Chinese parsley.

Coriander seeds are small, light brown and spherical, with tiny ribs that make it look like a Chinese lantern.

Aroma

Cilantro leaves, stems and roots have a fresh, grassy fragrance due to an organic compound that is also found in insects, which could be why some people are turned off by it. But don't let that stop you from using cilantro, as we have found that over 90% of the people we meet simply love it.

Coriander seeds are a completely different ball game. When they are dried, these little brown seeds develop a citrusy, warm and summer-hay-like aroma.

Flavor

Cilantro has a refreshing, lemony flavor that quickly diffuses, so it is always best added toward the end of cooking or used in dishes that are not cooked, to retain its flavor. Much like basil, it is almost impossible to use too much of this herb in a dish that is being cooked. You can use the stems and roots when finely chopped or grated, but they are not quite as bright in flavor.

Coriander seeds have an indistinct, savory-cracker-like, lemon-peel-and-dried-herb flavor that is far more useful than you would imagine. The flavor of coriander seeds amalgamates with that of other herbs, spices and foods. Almost any food that tends toward bitterness can be tamed with the liberal addition of ground coriander.

DRY ROASTING

This simple process changes the flavor to a deeper taste often preferred in curries.

Place whole seeds or powder in a semi-hot pan (just too hot to touch) and swirl the ingredient around until a nutty, toasted aroma is apparent.

Pairings

The clean, fresh and crisp profile of cilantro works well in Mexican, Asian and Indian cuisine. Cilantro pairs well with herbs like parsley, dill and basil, and spices such as chile, curry leaf, ginger, lemongrass and mint. Traditionally used with seafood and chicken, it's also a key contributor to the flavors of ceviche, salsas, stir-fries, Asian curries and Vietnamese Pho.

Coriander seed is a mainstay in blends as diverse as Indian and Asian curry powders, Moroccan tagine spices, garam masala and sweet mixed spices for cakes and cookies.

Cinnamon

One of the oldest spices mentioned in antiquity, cinnamon today is used in nearly every cuisine.

When shopping, you will see two types of cinnamon: whole or ground. The variety simply labeled cinnamon or Saigon cinnamon is native to southern China, Vietnam and Indonesia. A close relative is labeled as Sri Lankan or Ceylon cinnamon.

Both forms of cinnamon are harvested from tree bark. Although they're processed in different ways, the result of drying the bark creates the volatile oils that give cinnamon its characteristic aroma and flavor.

The cinnamon stick looks like a single mini scroll of thick bark that is quite hard. Cinnamon can be purchased in whole pieces, as sticks or in ground form. Ground cinnamon is very fine and dark brown to reddish-brown in color.

Aroma

Cinnamon has a sweet, somewhat pungent aroma that lingers and withstands the heat of cooking. No wonder it is so popular with bakers and donut makers, as they can rely on the wafting aroma of cinnamon to lure you in to purchase their baked goods.

Sri Lankan cinnamon has a milder sweet, warm aroma with pleasantly woody background notes. Its best quality is that it has no trace of sharpness or dominating pungency.

Flavor

Cinnamon's flavor is strong with a background bitterness and spicy heat that become apparent if you use too much.

Sri Lankan cinnamon has a milder, sweet and slightly woody cinnamon flavor with no bitterness or background heat.

Pairings

Both types of cinnamon pair well with all other spices, so they're found in spice blends such as sweet mixed spice, pumpkin pie spice, garam masala, curry powders for many cuisines, and even barbecue spice blends. Cinnamon sugar is easily made at home by blending 1 tsp cinnamon with 4 tsp (20 mL) granulated sugar.

Top of the list for traditional uses of this spice are cakes, sweet pastries and cookies. Whole cinnamon sticks are used to flavor stewed fruits and beverages like chai. Ground cinnamon is used in Moroccan tagines and sprinkled over baked pigeon pie. If you need to reduce your sugar consumption, try a sprinkle of Sri Lankan cinnamon on your oatmeal and other cereals, and you'll never miss sugar.

Cumin

Cumin seeds are the fruits of a small annual plant with delicate blue-green, frond-like leaves and slender stems. Harvesting in many countries is still performed by hand, as the plant is so fragile that mechanical methods are not practical. The seeds vary in color from pale brown to khaki with a fine, downy surface that makes them look dull. Cumin seeds must be threshed to remove a tiny "tail" that would not be desirable in food.

Ground cumin is an oily-textured, brown powder. The best quality tends to be dark in color, partly due to the practice of lightly roasting the seeds before grinding.

Black cumin is a different plant, and its seeds look a bit like small caraway seeds. Some stores sell "black cumin seed," which is actually nigella seed, and should not be used as a substitute for cumin seed.

Aroma

When you first smell cumin, curry comes immediately to mind, which is why it is often called the curry spice. But it does not stop there. Ground cumin releases more aroma than the whole seeds and has a warm, earthy and slightly minty fragrance that tends to linger. To me, it conjures up memories of spice markets in exotic locations and warehouses where hundreds of tons of cumin seeds are stored after harvest.

Flavor

Like the aroma of cumin, the taste is also a reminder of the flavor of curry. To me, the warm, slightly nutty and earthy taste of cumin makes it one of the great comfort-food spices. I believe this is because we have an inherent, subliminal instinct to not only identify with plants, but also with the earth that nourishes them.

Pairings

Cumin combines happily with most other spices, as it can balance and round out their sometimes-complex flavors.

One example of this characteristic is Mexican chili powder, which gets its unique taste from the addition of ground cumin. The traditional Egyptian blend of hazelnuts, pistachios and sesame seeds known as dukkah also contains ground cumin.

Cumin seeds are used in breads and rice dishes and when making pickles and chutneys. The spice also complements vegetables, such as carrots, squash and zucchini, and is even used to flavor some alcoholic liqueurs.

The most surprising pairing with cumin I've ever experienced was in Egypt, when I was given sweet shortbread cookies that contained whole cumin seeds. Absolutely delicious! It's what led me to experiment with cumin and sweetness in the form of honey.

In the same way that honey is delicious on a peanut butter sandwich, try sprinkling dukkah on a honey sandwich. The combination of sweet honey, nuts and the cumin in dukkah is a great surprise to spring on guests.

Fennel Seeds

Fennel is an annual herb plant with soft, frond-like foliage and a bulb at the base that is commonly used as a vegetable in recipes. The plant is native to (and still quite popular in) southern Europe and the Mediterranean, where it is called finocchio. In some shops, the fresh bulbs may be mislabeled as anise.

Fennel seeds are gathered after boisterous flowering, a lovely sight to behold. These seeds have been used for their bright, fresh flavor for centuries by the people of China, India, Egypt and Rome. These days, fennel seeds tend to be one of the most used but rarely acknowledged of all spices — always a bridesmaid but never the bride!

The seeds are yellow with a tinge of green; the greener the seed, the more intense the flavor. Seeds are ¼ inch (0.5 cm) long and you will notice that they often split in two, making them flat on one side and convex on the other. Pale, hair-width ribs run along the length of the seed, and sometimes they have a small stalk that's still intact.

Aroma

Fennel seeds have a slightly dry, hay-like note and a light licorice aroma, though not as pungent as anise seed or star anise. They all contain higher levels of anethol, the organic compound that is responsible for the aromas.

Flavor

The clean, bright taste of anise in fennel seeds is a favorite of mine, with warm, but not hot, spicy flavors. Indian restaurants generally have a dish of fennel seeds to chew after a meal to freshen your breath.

When dry-roasted, its flavor changes more than most spices. Other spices develop a deep, almost smoky flavor, while roasted fennel seeds are sweeter, almost as if light brown sugar had been added.

Pairings

Fennel seeds can combine well with all other spices, adding its bright profile to spice blends like curry powder, garam masala, Chinese five-spice powder, Cajun spice blend and Moroccan ras el hanout. Moreover, they are one of the must-have spices in Indian panch phoron, a ubiquitous blend of seed spices.

Fennel seeds are added to pickles, soups, breads, sausages, pasta and tomato dishes, as well as sauerkraut and salads. It's hard to imagine pork and fennel sausages without fennel seeds that complement the fattiness of pork so well. It is worth noting that spices with bright flavors balance the richness of foods like pork, duck and soft cheeses.

WHAT'S IN A NAME?

The name "fennel" is derived from the Roman word for "fragrant hay," *foeniculum*, which also gives us the botanical name of *Foeniculum vulgare*.

Fennel was a symbol of success in ancient Greece. In fact, it was referred to as "marathon" after the battleground on which the Greeks staged a victory over the Persians in 490 BCE.

Garlic

Belonging to the same family as onions, chives, leeks and shallots, garlic is a hardy perennial plant with firm, green leaves.

Garlic bulbs vary considerably in size, from small Asian ones to giant Californian varieties. The garlic bulb is a round lumpy collection of bulblets, called cloves, that are encased in a flaky parchment-like outer skin. When peeled and cut or minced, the enzymes within are activated and release a very strong aroma.

Fresh garlic can be purchased as whole bulbs, peeled cloves or in other semi-fresh forms, such as minced garlic and garlic paste in oil with preservatives.

Dried garlic is readily available as flakes or minced pieces and in powder form, usually labeled granulated garlic. These release their flavor easily into food and are convenient when just a small garlic hit is required.

Aroma

The aroma of fresh garlic when peeled or crushed is strong, sulfurous and lingering. You either love it or hate it.

Flavor

Sharp, acrid and hot is a good way to describe fresh garlic once the bulbs have been crushed, creating the compound allyl disulfide. When used sparingly, fresh garlic adds a pleasant piquancy to foods. A beginner cook may be surprised to find that, upon cooking, garlic develops quite a sweet flavor, without being overpowering. The flavor of roasted or barbecued garlic bulbs, when the soft, cooked cloves are squished out, is so appealing that you can eat these soft morsels on their own. What a contrast!

Pairings

Many herbs, spices and foods pair with it with great success. Garlic is found in most barbecue spices, Cajun seasonings, Italian herb and pizza mixes, and harissa, a North African paste. Another tasty vehicle for the herb is garlic butter, flavored with freshly crushed garlic and some finely chopped parsley, which accompanies foods such as seafood, artichoke hearts, avocados and asparagus. As a matter of fact, nearly every savory recipe can benefit from a hint of garlic.

Storage

When buying garlic, look for bulbs that hold together firmly, with no sign of the inner cloves shrinking away from the papery sheath. Garlic stores best when the bulbs are kept intact, as separated cloves lose their flavor more rapidly. Keep complete bulbs in an open container in a cool, dark place with low humidity.

GARLIC BREATH

Drink red wine with meals that contain garlic — the polyphenols in the wine break down the compounds that cause the smell to linger. Or try pairing parsley with garlic or chewing fennel seeds after a garlicky meal, both are thought to help sweeten one's breath.

Ginger

Ginger comes from the roots (rhizomes) of a tropical, perennial plant of the same name. Ginger could be easily transported while growing in pots on sea voyages; it was traded extensively and transplanted to many areas.

Gingerroot, as we commonly call it, comes fresh in knobby shaped pieces that are referred to in the spice trade as "hands," because of their knuckled, arthritic-looking shape.

Remove the papery skin before slicing, grating or crushing in a mortar and pestle. Simply scrape the skin off with a teaspoon. And there's no risk of cutting yourself by using a knife!

Ginger paste is made by crushing gingerroot and adding water and preservatives. Although convenient, it tends to compromise the true, fresh taste of ginger.

Preserved ginger is made by partially reducing the moisture content by salting, boiling and washing it, and then adding sugar syrup. Crystallized ginger is processed even more, by further boiling the gingerroot and then partially drying it and dusting it with sugar.

To make ground ginger, dried gingerroot is sliced, broken up into smaller pieces and ground to a fine, silky-smooth powder.

Aroma

Gingerroot has a sweet, slightly pungent aroma with a lemonlike freshness. Gingerroot that has been harvested when young is noticeably sweet and forms a smooth paste when grated. Older roots will have a sharper aroma; when grated, the paste has a high proportion of hairy fibers. Smell ground ginger before using it; if the aroma is sharp and makes you think of sneezing, use a bit less; it may be too strong.

Flavor

Bright, tangy, sweet, spicy and warm are the best ways to describe the taste of gingerroot. The taste of mature roots will be sharper and hotter than that of roots lifted when young.

During drying, gingerroot loses some of its fresh flavor notes; however, the taste becomes deeper and richer.

Pairings

Ginger adds freshness and zing to both sweet and savory recipes. Nearly all spice blends benefit from ginger, including Chinese five-spice powder, barbecue seasoning, Jamaican jerk seasoning and sweet pumpkin pie spice.

Ginger can tenderize meat; rub it on and let it marinate for a few hours in the refrigerator before cooking. Fishy, ammonia-like aromas associated with seafood can be greatly reduced by adding ginger and turmeric before cooking.

Storage

Gingerroot should not be peeled until using. Store the roots in an open container in a cupboard, the same way you would fresh onions and garlic. They should stay fresh for a week or two.

Mint touches our lives in so many ways. Looking for a breath freshener, mouthwash, toothpaste, chewing gum, cleaning agent? Mint will be there. And that's not even including all the culinary uses!

There are many members of the mint plant family, but the three main varieties we are talking about are spearmint, garden mint and peppermint.

Spearmint has deep-green, spear-shaped leaves and is the preferred variety when you want to grow your own mint plants. The dried mint you buy in stores is generally garden mint. It is almost identical to spearmint except that the leaves are rounder and somewhat crinkly. Peppermint has dark-green leaves, with its extract used mostly for flavoring baked goods, candy, drinks and toothpastes.

Aroma

Try to think of an aroma that says "cool'" and "fresh" more than that of mint — it is not easy. The herb's global appeal is driven by its bright, refreshing smell that comes from the essential oils, predominantly menthol, in its leaves. Peppermint's aroma is not quite as bright as spearmint, yet it has a deeper note due to the higher amount of menthol.

Flavor

The flavor of mint is similarly clean and fresh, a light taste that is not pungent or antiseptic-like. Fortunately, the agreeable flavor is conveniently captured in the cell structure of dried mint, making it a culinary favorite. Peppermint has a mild peppery bite and mouth-freshening germicidal characteristics, with a slight balsamic taste reminiscent of throat lozenges and mint candies.

Pairings

When many of us think of mint, the first dish that comes to mind is roast lamb with mint sauce. However, mint can also help reduce the richness of pork and goes equally well with veal and chicken. It's delicious sprinkled on steamed new potatoes or cooked green peas that have been tossed in a little butter. A little mint also pairs nicely with tomatoes and eggplant, or you can use the herb in cold cucumber soup or a fresh fruit salad, especially one with mangoes. Lastly, homemade oil and vinegar salad dressings can benefit from the addition of some fresh mint.

Middle Eastern, Moroccan, Indian and Asian cooking is enhanced by the inclusion of mint, including recipes such as stuffed vine leaves, tagine, butter chicken and stir-fried vegetables. A favorite of mine is the cooling cucumber, yogurt and mint sauce called raita, which gives perfect balance to spicy Indian meals.

Peppermint is mostly used at home for peppermint tea, a soothing, relaxing drink that can help clear head colds and aid in digestion. In cooking, the use of peppermint tends to be limited to sweet recipes like candies or cakes.

Oregano is a Mediterranean herb that is a close relative to the slightly milder-tasting herb marjoram, so it is sometimes called wild marjoram due to its robust character and vigorous growth. Another variety, true Mexican oregano, is a different species.

Dried oregano leaves, generally broken or rubbed, should be gray-green in color. Pale-brown leaves tend to have less flavor.

It can be confusing when shopping for this herb, as Mediterranean oregano can actually be grown in Mexico and is sometimes labeled as Mexican oregano, even though it is "normal" oregano. The true native Mexican oregano has a different aroma/flavor profile, so it is best to stick with the Mediterranean variety, which we'll simply call oregano, for our recipes.

Aroma

Fresh oregano has a classic herbaceous aroma and faint peppery freshness derived from its volatile oils. When dried, the more pungent, pepper-like smell becomes concentrated. When crushing a little in the palm of your hand, you will notice a warm, balsamic aroma.

Flavor

The flavor of fresh oregano is distinct, but not overpowering, so, like other fresh herbs, it can be used quite liberally. However, dried oregano is at least three to four times stronger by volume and has a faint bitter taste, so always use less than you would of fresh. Drying removes most of the moisture and concentrates those herby, peppery flavors.

Pairings

You could add oregano to most European recipes, as it relates perfectly to the food of that part of the world. Oregano complements basil nicely; the combination of these two herbs with liberal amounts of tomato has become synonymous with pizza and Italian pasta in most countries.

Oregano is excellent for enhancing dishes that contain eggplant, zucchini and bell pepper and is usually found in recipes for moussaka and meat loaf. If you want to give roast beef, lamb or pork full-bodied taste and a mouthwatering crust, rub the meat with a mixture of oregano, paprika and garlic powder before cooking. Lastly, when dried oregano is sprinkled over a feta and tomato salad with olives and capers, or used to garnish any meal, the effect is not dissimilar to grinding black pepper over your food, adding that fresh punch of herb just before serving.

Oregano is compatible with all other herbs when used in minor proportions, so it does not overpower a dish. It features in numerous herb and spice blends, including Italian herbs (of course!), mixed herbs, seasonings for meat, turkey stuffing mixes, bouquet garni and herbes de Provence. When you have oregano in the kitchen, you will always find a use for it.

Paprika

Paprika is a direct descendant of the most common variety of chile, *Capsicum annuum*. Paprika has very low levels of capsaicin, the active component that makes chiles hot.

Hungarians needed to differentiate the spice from chile, so they named it paprika, which denotes this universally appealing fruit, which is similar to a red bell pepper.

Harvested paprika were traditionally hung up to dry on strings (*ristras*) and then ground to a fine powder. There are four main styles:

Mild paprika is dark red, rich in flavor and has a slightly bitter taste that goes well in Spanish and Moroccan dishes.

Sweet paprika is most commonly from Hungary, and has a sweet, fruity taste with no sharpness or bitterness at all.

Smoked paprika is made by smoking the pods as part of the drying and curing process.

Hot paprika is made from pods that have some capsaicin content; on a heat scale, they might be like a mild chile.

Aroma

Both Spaniards and Hungarians developed an enduring love of paprika for its brilliant color and appetizing aroma. Imagine a dried red bell pepper — warm, comforting and vaguely earthy. Sweet paprika powder has an aroma like a dried chile de arbol, while smoked sweet paprika has a distinct wood-smoked aroma.

Flavor

Ripe fruits have higher naturally occurring sugar content than unripe ones, making them sweeter. When dried, the flavor becomes deep and rich, like the taste of a sun-dried tomato. Good-quality sweet paprika should be bright red without any bitter background taste. Some mild, dark-colored types of paprika will have a slight bitter note, so they should be used more sparingly. Smoked sweet paprika has a stronger flavor, so if substituting it for sweet, use about one-third of the amount.

Pairings

Paprika is one of the most useful spices to have in the pantry, as even the simplest of foods can gain color and flavor from its use. Paprika is always used ground, making it a convenient spice to keep on hand.

Mild paprika has a rich flavor and a slightly sharp aftertaste that goes well with other spices like cumin, fennel seed, ginger, oregano and thyme. It's used widely in roasts and Moroccan tagines.

Sweet paprika is the best to use with seafood, chicken, veal and vegetables. It is the go-to paprika when making Hungarian goulash and it makes a beautiful and tasty garnish.

Smoked paprika is stronger and pairs nicely with red meat and slow-cooked dishes. It can be blended 50/50 with sweet paprika to give it a pleasant flavor kick without being too intense.

Storage

Paprika is very prone to degradation from constant exposure to light. Store it in a very dark place.

Rosemary

Rosemary is a hardy shrub that loves to be in the sun. There is an upright variety, which is most commonly used in cooking, and a prostrate variety with smaller leaves and pale-blue flowers. Both have the same flavor.

Fresh rosemary leaves are needlelike, dark green and glossy on top with a long crease down the middle. Underneath the leaf is grey-green, and the edges look as if they are neatly rolled. Upon drying, the leaves curl tightly and look like hard, little pine needles.

Native to the Mediterranean, rosemary gets its name from the Latin words *ros* (dew) and *marinos* (sea), or "dew of the sea," in reference to the areas in the Mediterranean where it grows so abundantly.

Rosemary's stimulating and health-giving properties are well documented. Hair rinses containing rosemary are said to promote vigor and growth, and Greek scholars used to wear sprigs of rosemary in their hair to help them commit their studies to memory.

Aroma

Upon being crushed, fresh rosemary leaves yield a strong fragrance that is pine-like and cooling with a minty, eucalyptus-like freshness that is distinctly head-clearing. Once dried, the leaves retain their pine scent but it's not as refreshing as that of fresh rosemary.

Flavor

The taste of fresh rosemary is quite pungent and bright, while the dried leaves are slightly woody, pine-like and refreshing, almost minty.

Pairings

It is somewhat surprising that such a strong-tasting herb should be so useful and versatile.

The astringent, crisp and savory taste of rosemary complements starchy foods, so it is delicious in dumplings, breads and savory cookies. Speaking of starchy foods, adding ½ tsp of finely chopped fresh rosemary to mashed potatoes or legumes is a treat, and including a sprig of fresh rosemary will enhance most casseroles.

The herb also counters the richness in liver pâté and in meats such as pork, lamb, duck and game. One of my favorite basic meals is a leg of lamb with sprigs of rosemary and slivers of garlic stuffed into slits in the meat, liberally dusted with sweet paprika before roasting.

Rosemary's powerful flavor does not overpower a dish when it is matched with other strong ingredients, such as garlic or wine. Even vegetables such as zucchini, eggplant, Brussels sprouts and cabbage are all enlivened by the fresh, resinous taste of rosemary.

We usually advise against using powdered herbs; in most cases, grinding leaves finely causes the flavors to dissipate rapidly. However, with its high oil content, rosemary is an exception. Because the dried leaves are quite hard and take a long time to soften in cooking, ground rosemary is an effective, convenient way to get the best results. Ground rosemary makes all the difference to lamb chops and other red meats when it is rubbed on with a little salt before grilling.

Thyme is a small, bushy and stiff-branched perennial shrub with tiny, narrow and gray-green leaves. The thyme we use commonly in cooking is called common or garden thyme. Although there are nearly 100 types of thyme, most are decorative and grown for their appearance rather than for use in cooking.

Thyme is native to the Mediterranean and North Africa, and its name comes from the Greek *thymon*, which means to fumigate. In the Middle East, thyme is known as za'atar, not to be confused with the blend of thyme, sesame, sumac and salt by the same name that you might find at the grocery store.

The herb has become a mainstay in most cuisines, though it is rarely seen in Asian recipes.

Lemon thyme plants, which have a slight lemony fragrance and flavor, are available from plant nurseries, while dried lemon thyme is sometimes sold in specialty stores.

Aroma

Fresh thyme has a bright, strong and agreeable aroma that conjures up memories of roast turkey stuffing and hearty winter dishes. Don't be put off by the reference to fumigation above, as it was a common practice to use fragrant herbs as air freshener before the invention of artificial room deodorizers. No matter what the marketers say, we always prefer natural aromas like thyme.

Flavor

The flavor is similarly strong, minty and warm, with dried thyme having more pungency than fresh leaves. Its citrusy, mouth-freshening taste, with a slight spicy sharpness, tends to linger. Because of its similarity, oregano is often combined with thyme or used as a substitute.

Pairings

Thyme can be found in many Western and Middle Eastern recipes due to its distinctive savory pungency that brings a depth of flavor to soups, stews and almost any dish that contains meat.

This herb is traditionally added to a bouquet garni (a bunch of herbs made up of thyme, oregano, parsley and bay leaves) and the classic mixed herbs blend (consisting of thyme, sage and oregano). The French blend herbes de Provence contains thyme, along with lavender and other herbs. You can also find thyme in Cajun and Jamaican jerk spice blends.

Thyme complements the flavor of chicken really nicely. One of our favorite ways to cook chicken is to coat pieces with a za'atar blend prior to grilling, pan-frying or baking. Thyme is excellent in pâtés and terrines, meat loaf, ground beef and sausages.

The herb also loves vegetables. It adds a delicious savoriness to mushrooms pan-fried in butter, and has an affinity for tomatoes and potatoes — it's especially effective in flavoring potato salad and a mixture of corn and green beans.

It works well in rich sauces and gravies, plus it is an important infusing ingredient when making pickles and flavoring spiced olives.

Turmeric

Turmeric roots are rhizomes, the part that grows off the primary tuber of a plant. Turmeric is a close relative to ginger, but there's not much similarity beyond that connection. Turmeric roots are orange-yellow in color when fresh, and bright to deep yellow when dried. In dried form, the roots are extremely hard and almost impossible to grind at home, which is why the spice is mostly sold as a powder.

Ground turmeric will vary in color, from pale yellow through to a darker, richer-looking ochre. That's why the spice is used extensively as a coloring in foods in response to increasing consumer demand for natural colors.

Turmeric contains curcumin, a naturally occurring compound that has scientifically confirmed, health-giving properties, primarily as an anti-inflammatory. It's been used for centuries in the Indian alternative medicine system known as ayurveda and in other forms of traditional medicine.

Ground turmeric has a higher curcumin content by weight than fresh turmeric. To maximize its bioactivity, the powder should be consumed with at least 10% ground black pepper. Note that pale-yellow turmeric powder has around 2.5% curcumin, while the darker-colored powders may have up to 6.5% of the compound.

Aroma

Fresh turmeric has a faintly earthy smell, as well as a slight gingery freshness combined with light mint and citrus notes, like those found in gingerroot.

Flavor

The taste of fresh turmeric is quite mild and minty, but it becomes stronger and more concentrated after drying. Ground turmeric powder is one of the most surprising spices when it comes to its flavor. The taste is earthy, a little metallic and bitter, reminiscent of black pepper, but when combined with almost any other spice or food, it comes alive by helping balance the other flavors.

Pairings

For many years, turmeric's most common use was as a food coloring. It is still employed to make pickles and relishes yellow and is often added to rice as a coloring substitute for saffron (without the same flavor, of course). Turmeric was sometimes used as filler in curry powder to reduce costs. However, turmeric is no longer a low-cost spice used for bulk and color, partly due to its increasing popularity as a health supplement.

Although most associated with curries, turmeric is also a vital ingredient in Moroccan and Asian dishes. One popular, golden-colored prawn dish (prawn moilee) from south India is spiced simply with turmeric, chile, ginger and cilantro.

Allspice, chile, cilantro, coriander seed, garlic, ginger and paprika all combine particularly well with turmeric.
If you find strong fishy aromas unpleasant, turmeric, along with ginger, is a spice that can greatly reduce the smells of robust, oily seafood.

It's time to start cooking! Here are some basic recipes, with simple variations, called Flavor Change-Ups, to give you an appreciation of the transformative power that herbs and spices have to shift a dish's flavor profile with ease.

To get started:

- *Choose the basic recipe you'd like to try:* Skillet Chicken Breast with Pan Sauce (page 52), Classic Pot Roast (page 54), Salmon Parcels (page 56), or Crispy Fried Tofu (page 58).
- *Choose a Flavor Change-Up:* Each recipe offers four different ways to change the flavor profile of the recipe, simply by changing the dominant herb or spice.

Try the Skillet Chicken Breast with a sweet paprika Flavor Change-Up. Then try it with fresh basil. Or bake Salmon Parcels with sweet allspice and then again with fiery chile. Once you get used to how each ingredient changes the flavor of a recipe, you can start experimenting with other spices and herbs.

As you gain knowledge and confidence in the kitchen, go even further and try the 60 easy-to-make dishes in the recipe section starting on page 63.

1 TEASPOON

Skillet Chicken Breast with Pan Sauce

This beginner-friendly recipe transforms simple chicken breasts into a delicious weeknight meal, complete with a sauce made in the same pan. It's a great recipe to show how easy it is to change the flavor profile of a dish by making small changes in the herbs or spices. Perfect for weeknights, try it with buttered boiled potatoes and green beans.

Makes 2 servings

TIP

For perfectly cooked chicken, use a meat thermometer. Insert it into the thickest part of the chicken and ensure it reads 165°F (74°C) before serving.

1 tbsp olive oil

1 tbsp butter

½ tsp salt , plus more as needed

¼ tsp freshly ground black pepper, plus more as needed

2 (10 to 14 oz/300 to 400 g) boneless skinless chicken breasts

½ cup (125 mL) ready-to-use chicken broth

1. Heat olive oil and butter in a large skillet over medium heat until butter melts and begins to foam.

2. Sprinkle ½ tsp salt and ¼ tsp pepper on chicken breasts.

3. Add chicken to the skillet and cook until golden brown, about 3 minutes per side (chicken will not be fully cooked). Transfer to a plate.

4. Pour chicken broth into the skillet, stirring to combine with the browned bits.

5. Turn heat to medium-low; return chicken to the skillet and cook until no longer pink inside (an internal temperature of 165°F/74°C; see tip), 3 to 4 minutes per side. Season to taste with additional salt and pepper.

6. Transfer each chicken breast to a plate; spoon pan sauce over chicken.

FLAVOR CHANGE-UPS

PAPRIKA

Sweet paprika adds warm, earthy flavors to the chicken. *Alternative serving suggestion:* Mashed potatoes and wilted spinach.

- Combine 1 tbsp mild or sweet paprika with 2 tbsp (30 mL) all-purpose flour, ¼ tsp salt, and a pinch of freshly ground black pepper in a shallow bowl.
- Follow the recipe above, but replace step 2 by coating chicken breasts in paprika mixture before cooking.

OREGANO

Dried oregano and fresh lemon juice lend an herbaceous, tangy touch of the Mediterranean to this chicken dish. *Alternative serving suggestion:* Oven fries and a dressed romaine salad.

- Follow the recipe above, but in step 2, sprinkle 1 tsp dried oregano and ¼ tsp salt over each side of chicken.
- Add 2 tbsp (30 mL) lemon juice along with the chicken broth in step 4.

GINGER

A combination of gingerroot, honey and soy sauce brings classic Asian flavors to the dish. *Alternative serving suggestion:* Steamed jasmine rice and broccoli.

- In step 1, add 1 tbsp freshly minced gingerroot to the skillet along with the butter and oil.
- In step 4, stir in 1 tbsp honey and 2 tbsp (30 mL) soy sauce with the chicken broth.

BASIL

Fresh basil and sweet cherry tomatoes add a burst of Italian inspiration to this staple chicken recipe. *Alternative serving suggestion:* Pasta shells tossed with olive oil and arugula.

- In step 4, add 10 cherry tomatoes, halved, to the skillet with the broth.
- In step 5, add 20 torn basil leaves to the skillet along with the chicken.

A pot roast is a wonderful recipe to have in your repertoire. It uses a flavorsome but economical cut of beef that slow-cooks to perfection. Cooking the dish "low and slow" ensures a result that's both tender and delicious. The thyme provides a pleasing aroma without an overpowering flavor. Crusty bread and buttered peas are the perfect accompaniments.

Makes 2 servings

Preheat oven to 325°F (160°C)

Dutch oven

- 3 tsp all-purpose flour
- 1 tsp salt
- ½ tsp freshly ground black pepper
- 1 (1 lb/500 g) chuck steak
- 1 tbsp olive oil
- 1 onion, halved and sliced
- 1 large clove garlic, minced
- ¾ cup (175 mL) ready-to-use beef broth
- ¾ cup (175 mL) water
- 1 tsp tomato paste
- 1 sprig fresh thyme
- About 7 oz (210 g) potatoes, cut into 2-inch (5 cm) pieces
- About 3½ oz (105 g) carrot, cut into 1-inch (2.5 cm) slices

1. In a shallow dish, combine flour, salt and pepper. Coat both sides of steak evenly with mixture.
2. Heat oil on the stovetop in Dutch oven over medium-high heat. Sear steak until browned, 4 minutes per side. Turn heat to low, and transfer steak to a plate.
3. Add onion and garlic to Dutch oven, stirring until softened, about 2 minutes. Add broth, ¾ cup (175 mL) water, tomato paste and thyme, scraping the bottom of Dutch oven with a spoon to incorporate any flavorful browned bits.
4. Return steak to Dutch oven and bring to a simmer. Cover with a tight-fitting lid and transfer to preheated oven. Bake for 60 minutes.
5. Remove Dutch oven from oven, turn steak over and add potatoes and carrots, arranging them around the edges (they do not need to be submerged). Cover and return to oven for 60 minutes.
6. Steak is done when the meat easily falls apart with a fork.
7. Remove the thyme. Divide steak and vegetables between two shallow bowls and pour sauce evenly over the top.

FLAVOR CHANGE-UPS

THYME

Thyme and red wine give a French-inspired twist to this pot roast with extra herbaceous depth.

- In step 3, add ½ cup (125 mL) dry red wine after cooking the onion. Stir for 1 minute to burn off the alcohol and then add broth, water and tomato paste. Add 3 sprigs of thyme instead of 1.
- In step 5, omit carrots and add about 3½ oz (105 g) button mushrooms, halved, at the same time as the potatoes.

CUMIN

This variation introduces a unique earthy warmth to this classic dinner.

- In step 1, add ½ tsp ground cumin to the flour mixture.
- In step 3, stir in ½ tsp whole cumin seeds with the onion and garlic. Increase tomato paste to 2 tsp.

ROSEMARY

Adding the brightness of rosemary and citrus to this pot roast will make your kitchen smell like springtime.

- In step 3, add ½ cup (125 mL) dry white wine after cooking the onion. Stir for 1 minute to burn off the alcohol. Omit tomato paste and add 1 sprig of fresh rosemary (or 1 tbsp dried rosemary) along with the broth and water.
- In step 7, cut ½ lemon into quarters and serve alongside vegetables.

PAPRIKA

For smoky, earthy notes reminiscent of bacon, try using smoked paprika to flavor this dish.

- In step 1, add ½ tsp smoked paprika to flour mixture.
- In step 3, stir an additional ½ tsp smoked paprika into broth.
- In step 5, omit carrots and add 1 red bell pepper, cut into thin strips.

Salmon Parcels

Cooking salmon in parchment paper locks in moisture and flavor, creating a dish that is both easy and nutritious. This method allows the fish and vegetables in the recipe to steam together, resulting in very tender and tasty results. Each variation offers a unique twist, from aromatic spices to fresh herbs.

Makes 2 servings

Preheat oven to 350°F (180°C)

2 pieces of parchment paper, approximately 16 by 12 inches (40 by 30 cm) each

2 salmon fillets (5 oz/150 g each)

1 lemon, cut into 6 slices

8 asparagus spears, trimmed

½ tsp salt

¼ tsp freshly ground black pepper

1. Place each salmon fillet, skin side down, in the center of a piece of parchment.
2. Arrange 3 slices of lemon on top of each salmon fillet and 2 asparagus spears on each side. Sprinkle with salt and pepper.
3. Bring long sides of parchment together and fold over to seal. Tightly fold the short edges, while leaving enough space inside parcel for salmon to steam.
4. Place parcels on a baking sheet and bake in preheated oven for 12 minutes.
5. Transfer parcels directly onto plates for diners to open themselves.

FLAVOR CHANGE-UPS

ALLSPICE

Introduce some sweetness to this salmon dish using ground allspice.

- In step 2, add ¼ tsp allspice to each salmon fillet before placing lemon slices on top. Replace asparagus with 6 trimmed green beans per parcel.

GINGER

Create an Asian-inspired dish with gingerroot, bok choy and soy sauce.

- In step 2, omit lemon. Thinly slice a 2-inch (5 cm) piece of ginger and place slices on top of salmon. Omit asparagus and add 1 halved piece of baby bok choy per parcel. Add 1 tsp soy sauce to each fillet before sealing parcels.

BASIL

Give the salmon a fresh and summery Italian touch with basil and tomatoes.

- In step 2, place 3 fresh basil leaves underneath lemon slices on each fillet. Omit asparagus and add 8 halved cherry tomatoes per parcel.
- In step 5, cut open each parcel and sprinkle an extra 3 torn basil leaves over the salmon before serving.

CHILE

Add some smoky heat with Mexican chipotle chile and a zesty lime twist.

- In step 2, spread $\frac{1}{4}$ tsp chipotle paste or sprinkle $\frac{1}{4}$ tsp ground chipotle powder on each fillet. Omit lemon and add 2 lime slices per fillet. Omit asparagus and divide $\frac{1}{2}$ cup (125 mL) fresh or frozen corn kernels between parcels.
- In step 5, cut open parcels and sprinkle each with 1 tbsp chopped cilantro, if desired.

Crispy Fried Tofu

Tofu is a versatile, plant-based protein that, when prepared correctly, can become the star of any meal. This recipe focuses on creating golden, crispy tofu with minimal effort, perfect for pairing with salads, rice or dipping sauces. The key to success is removing as much moisture as possible before cooking. Serve this tofu on shredded lettuce with ranch dressing for a simple yet satisfying dish.

Makes 2 servings

TIP

A tofu press is invaluable for frequent tofu preparation, helping to remove moisture efficiently. If you don't have one, wrap the tofu in a clean dishcloth, place a heavy object (like a skillet or hardcover book) on top of it for 15 minutes, remove from dishcloth and then blot dry with a paper towel.

1 block (14 oz/400 g) firm tofu, pressed to remove moisture (see tip)

¼ cup (60 mL) cornstarch

Salt

½ tsp garlic powder

Vegetable oil, for frying

1. Cut tofu into 1-inch (2.5 cm) cubes.
2. In a medium bowl, combine cornstarch, 1 tsp salt and garlic powder. Gently toss tofu cubes in the mixture, ensuring each piece is evenly coated and any excess is shaken off.
3. Heat a skillet over medium-high heat and add enough vegetable oil to cover the bottom by 1⁄16 inch (2 mm).
4. Once oil starts to form small bubbles, use tongs to carefully place tofu cubes in the skillet without crowding (cook in batches if necessary). Fry until golden and crispy, 3 minutes on each side.
5. Transfer tofu to paper towel to drain excess oil. Sprinkle with additional salt, if desired, and serve warm.

FLAVOR CHANGE-UPS

CHILE

To give this tofu treat a slightly spicy and smoky flavor, add warming spices to the coating mixture.

- In step 2, add ¼ tsp cayenne pepper and ½ tsp smoked paprika to cornstarch mixture.

OREGANO

Infuse this tofu dish some Mediterranean flair with the addition of oregano and a citrusy finish.

- In step 2, add 1 tsp dried oregano to cornstarch mixture.
- In step 5, after draining tofu on paper towel, squeeze the juice of half a lemon over it.

CUMIN

Incorporate whole cumin seeds into this recipe for a nutty crunch and aromatic profile—perfect for pairing with fried rice.

- In step 2, add 1 tsp whole cumin seeds to cornstarch mixture.

MINT

Freshen up your tofu with dried mint, ideal for serving with yogurt-based dressings or dips.

- In step 2, add 1 tsp dried mint leaves to cornstarch mixture.

The Spice & Herb Recipes

The following recipes are organized alphabetically by the featured spice. All the ingredients are easy to find at most grocery stores and the step-by-step instructions are simple enough for any level of cooking skill.

You'll quickly see as you make each one how the spices and herbs create layers of flavor that will satisfy your palate, and even wow your friends and family.

Jerk-Style Chicken Thighs

It's no surprise that Jamaican native allspice is the hero in jerk marinade. Combined with herbaceous thyme and fiery chile, this is a mouthwatering marinade with delicious results. Enjoy in a wrap or as a chicken burger, shredded in a grain bowl or with Cilantro and Black Bean Salsa (see page 82).

Makes 4 servings

Preheat oven to 340°F (170°C)

Food processor

Baking sheet, lined with parchment paper

1 onion, chopped

1 Scotch bonnet or other small hot chile

1 large clove garlic

1 tbsp packed brown sugar

1 tsp salt

1 tsp dried thyme

1½ tsp ground allspice

2 tbsp (30 mL) neutral oil (such as canola or vegetable)

1 lb (500 g) skinless boneless chicken thighs (about 4 medium thighs)

1. In food processor, combine onion, chile, garlic, brown sugar, salt, thyme, allspice and oil. Process until smooth.
2. Place chicken thighs in a medium bowl. Add marinade and toss until evenly coated. Transfer chicken to prepared baking sheet, smooth side up.
3. Bake in preheated oven for 60 minutes or until juices run clear when chicken is pierced (see tip). Do not flip during cooking.
4. Let stand for 5 minutes before serving.

TIPS

For bone-in skin-on thighs (about 1½ lbs/750 g), increase cooking time by 15 minutes.

Marinate chicken for up to 2 days for more flavor.

Leftover chicken can be shredded, cooled and placed in an airtight container in freezer for up to 3 months.

Simple Swedish Meatballs

A beloved comfort food classic, Swedish meatballs are known for their warm spices and creamy sauce. This recipe pairs a mix of pork and beef with allspice and a touch of Dijon mustard for depth of flavor. Serve over egg noodles or with mashed potatoes for a satisfying meal.

Makes about 20 meatballs (4 servings)

MEATBALLS

5 oz (150 g) ground pork

5 oz (150 g) ground beef

1 large egg, beaten

¼ cup (60 mL) dry bread crumbs

½ tsp garlic powder

½ tsp salt

⅓ tsp ground allspice

Pinch freshly ground black pepper

Pinch dried oregano

SAUCE

1 tbsp unsalted butter

2 tbsp (30 mL) all-purpose flour

1½ cups (375 mL) ready-to-use chicken broth

½ cup (125 mL) sour cream

¼ tsp Dijon mustard

¼ tsp ground allspice

Additional salt and freshly ground black pepper

1. *Meatballs:* In a large bowl, thoroughly combine pork, beef, egg, bread crumbs, garlic powder, ½ tsp salt, allspice, pinch black pepper and oregano. Roll mixture into golf ball–sized meatballs (about 1½ inches/4 cm in diameter).

2. Heat a deep skillet over medium heat. Add meatballs and brown them, turning occasionally, for 10 minutes. No oil is necessary, as the fat will render during cooking. Transfer meatballs to a plate and set aside. Meatballs will not be cooked through yet.

3. *Sauce:* In the same skillet, over low heat, add butter and flour. Stir constantly for 1 minute to cook flour.

4. Gradually whisk in chicken broth to form a smooth sauce, keeping on low heat. Add sour cream, mustard and allspice. Stir well to combine.

5. Return meatballs to the skillet. Simmer, stirring occasionally, until meatballs are cooked through and sauce has thickened, about 15 minutes.

6. Season sauce to taste with additional salt and pepper before serving.

TIP

Uncooked meatballs can be stored in the refrigerator for 1 day before cooking, or frozen for up to 3 months.

Allspice Apple Teatime Cake

Lightly spiced apple cake is perfect for a treat in the morning or afternoon. The warm flavor of allspice pairs beautifully with the natural sweetness of apples, much the way cinnamon does, but with a little more depth.

Makes one 9-inch (23 cm) cake

Preheat oven to 350°F (180°C)

9-inch (23 cm) cake pan, greased

Electric stand mixer or portable mixer

FRAGRANT VANILLA

We don't cover vanilla in this book, but it's a widely used, much-revered spice. Vanilla comes from the bean of a tropical orchid, which is dried and cured before use. Make sure you always buy vanilla *extract* not *essence*, as essence may simply be artificial.

CAKE

½ cup (125 mL) superfine (caster) sugar (see tip, page 79)

¼ cup (60 mL) butter, softened

1 egg

1¼ cups (310 mL) all-purpose flour

1 tsp baking powder

½ tsp ground allspice

6 tbsp (90 mL) milk

1 large cooking apple (see tip), peeled, cored and cut into ½-inch (1 cm) cubes

TOPPING

1 tbsp superfine (caster) sugar

½ tsp ground allspice

1 tbsp butter, melted

1. *Cake:* In a mixing bowl, beat sugar and butter with electric mixer at high speed until light and fluffy. Add egg and mix on low until just combined.
2. Gradually mix in flour, baking powder and allspice.
3. Add milk, 1 to 2 tbsp (15 to 30 mL) at a time, mixing until batter reaches dropping consistency (see tip).
4. Pour batter into prepared cake pan. Top evenly with cubed apple, pressing the fruit gently into batter.
5. Bake in the preheated oven for 20 to 25 minutes, until browned on top and a skewer inserted into the center comes out clean.
6. Let cool in the pan for about 5 minutes. Turn cake out onto a wire rack and cool for 5 minutes.
7. *Topping:* In a small bowl, combine sugar and allspice. Brush top of cake with melted butter, then sprinkle topping mixture evenly over it.
8. Serve warm or store in an airtight container for up to 3 days and serve cold.

TIPS

For the best results, use cooking apples such as Granny Smith, Honeycrisp or Jonagold.

Dropping consistency: Batter should fall easily from a spoon into the bowl within seconds.

Roasted Allspice Sweet Potato

This warmly spiced side dish highlights the natural sugar content of sweet potatoes with a tangy touch of lime and the layered depth of allspice. Perfect served warm as an accompaniment for grilled meats and fresh salads.

Makes 4 servings

Preheat oven to 350°F (180°C)

Baking sheet, lined with parchment paper

1 tbsp olive oil

1 tbsp lime juice

1 tsp brown sugar

½ tsp ground allspice

Pinch salt

2 (1⅓ lb/600 g) sweet potatoes, skin on, halved lengthwise

1. In a small bowl, combine oil, lime juice, brown sugar, allspice and salt until smooth.
2. Place sweet potatoes, cut side up, on the prepared baking sheet. Using a sharp knife, score (see tip) the cut side of each sweet potato diagonally into a grid pattern, spacing lines ½ inch (1 cm) apart.
3. Divide oil mixture evenly over cut sides of sweet potatoes, ensuring full coverage.
4. Roast in preheated oven for 45 minutes or until sweet potatoes are soft, and the tops are browned.

TIP

Scoring (making shallow incisions) allows any flavorings to penetrate more deeply while cooking.

VARIATION

Cut sweet potato into 1-inch (2.5 cm) cubes and reduce the cooking time to 25 minutes. Use these potatoes in salads or grain bowls.

Lemon, Crab and Basil Linguine

Sometimes an elegant restaurant-quality dish is surprisingly simple to make at home. The secret lies in using the freshest, highest-quality ingredients you can find. In this recipe, the basil is an important element in bringing the flavors together. Serve with Watermelon, Haloumi and Mint Salad (page 120) for the ultimate summer lunch.

Makes 2 servings

1 tbsp extra virgin olive oil

2 large cloves garlic, crushed

1 long red chile, seeded and very finely diced (see tip)

3½ oz (105 g) cooked backfin (lump) crabmeat (see tip)

2 tsp finely grated lemon zest

15 basil leaves, torn

Salt and freshly ground black pepper

7 oz (210 g) linguine

1. Bring a large pot of salted water to a boil over high heat.
2. Meanwhile, in a small skillet, heat oil over medium heat. Add garlic and cook until fragrant, about 1 minute. Stir in chile, crabmeat, lemon zest, basil, ½ tsp salt and ½ tsp black pepper. Cook for 1 minute, stirring well. Remove from heat.
3. Add linguine to boiling water and cook according to package instructions. When nearly done, reserve ¼ cup (60 mL) of pasta water and add it to the skillet with crab mixture.
4. Drain cooked pasta and return it to the pot. Add crab mixture and toss well with tongs to coat pasta evenly. Season to taste with additional salt and pepper. Serve immediately.

Tips

Use fresh crabmeat for the best flavor, or canned crab (drained well) if fresh isn't available.

If you prefer a spicier kick, leave the seeds in the chile.

The Only Pesto Recipe You Will EVER Need

This fresh, pungent pesto is made with fragrant basil, toasted pine nuts and rich Parmesan cheese. Serve it tossed in hot pasta, combine with additional oil for a salad dressing or whisk into eggs before scrambling. Traditionally, pesto was roughly mixed in a mortar with a pestle, but a food processor is an efficient, much easier way to do it now. Because of the fine blending, you don't need to remove the leaves from the stems, as they contain just as much flavor!

Makes 4 to 6 servings

Food processor

WHAT IS A MORTAR AND PESTLE?

A pestle is a heavy tool (like half a rolling pin) and a mortar is a solid bowl. Both are usually made from a heavy material, such as stone or metal. In ancient times, this was the only method for milling or grinding. This set of tools is still commonly used to create a coarse powder (like when we grind spices) or a rough paste (like pesto).

2 cups (500 mL) tightly packed fresh basil leaves and stems

½ cup (125 mL) pine nuts, lightly toasted (see tip)

½ cup (125 mL) coarsely chopped Parmesan cheese

2 cloves garlic, minced

½ tsp finely grated lemon zest

½ tsp fine sea salt

¼ tsp freshly ground black pepper

⅓ cup (75 mL) extra virgin olive oil

1. In food processor fitted with the metal blade, add basil, pine nuts, Parmesan, garlic, lemon zest, salt and pepper.

2. With the motor running, pour oil through the feed tube and process until pesto mixture is puréed but retains some texture.

3. Serve immediately or store for later (see tip).

TIPS

To toast pine nuts, cook them in a dry skillet over medium heat, shaking the pan lightly, until lightly golden, about 2 minutes. Remove skillet from heat as soon as pine nuts start to color.

Pesto will keep in an airtight container in the refrigerator for up to 2 weeks, as long as the top is covered with $\frac{1}{16}$ inch (2 mm) olive oil to prevent oxidation. Pesto can also be frozen—ice cube trays are great for freezing single portions for pasta. Simply drain cooked pasta, reserving a little cooking liquid, then stir through the pesto and it will melt in moments.

For a runnier pesto, add ¼ cup (60 mL) water with the oil. This is good for using as a salad dressing.

VARIATION

Replace 1 cup (250 mL) basil with baby spinach for a nutrition-packed pesto.

Roasted Tomato and Basil Soup

Basil and tomato are a classic culinary partnership. As you've read, basil leaves and allspice berries share a common compound, eugenol, making allspice a natural addition to this recipe. This soup is delicious served with warm, crusty garlic bread.

Makes 4 servings

Preheat the oven to 200°F (100°C)

Baking sheet, lined with parchment

Immersion blender

2 lbs (1 kg) ripe tomatoes, halved

2 large cloves garlic, peeled

1 tsp dried basil

1 tsp sea salt

½ tsp ground allspice

2 tsp extra virgin olive oil, plus more to serve

3 cups (750 mL) ready-to-use vegetable or chicken broth

1 tbsp tomato paste

10 leaves fresh basil, plus more for garnish (optional)

1. Place the tomatoes and garlic on the baking sheet. Sprinkle with dried basil, sea salt and allspice, then drizzle with the olive oil. Roast in preheated oven for 2 hours or until very soft.
2. Bring the broth to a simmer on the stove, and once the tomatoes are roasted, add them with roasted garlic to the broth. Stir in tomato paste and fresh basil. Bring the soup to a boil, then reduce the heat and simmer for 5 minutes.
3. Remove the soup from the heat. Let cool slightly, then purée in blender or directly in the pan using a immersion blender.
4. Serve with additional oil and a fresh basil leaf if desired.

TIP

This soup can be served hot or chilled, but it is best enjoyed at room temperature to fully appreciate its flavor.

VARIATION

For a creamy soup, replace 1 cup (250 mL) of broth with light (5%) cream, and add it at the end of Step 2 (it will split if overheated).

Peach and Basil Bruschetta

This bruschetta is the epitome of summer, balancing the sweetness of ripe peaches with creamy mozzarella and fresh, aromatic basil.

Makes 2 to 4 servings

1 cup (250 mL) diced ripe peach (¼-inch/0.5 cm)

4½ oz (140 g) buffalo mozzarella, cut into ½-inch (1 cm) cubes

15 fresh basil leaves, roughly chopped or torn

1½ tbsp extra-virgin olive oil, divided

Salt and freshly ground black pepper

4 (¾-inch/2 cm) slices ciabatta bread

1. In a medium bowl, combine peach, mozzarella, basil, 1 tbsp olive oil, and a pinch each of salt and pepper. Stir thoroughly. Let mixture stand for at least 10 minutes or up to 60 minutes to allow the flavors to develop.

2. Brush both sides of ciabatta slices with remaining olive oil. Heat a griddle pan or large skillet over medium-high heat and toast the ciabatta until crisp and golden, about 2 minutes per side.

3. Top each piece of toasted ciabatta with peach mixture. Finish with an extra grind of pepper (see tip). Serve immediately.

TIP

For an extra layer of flavor, drizzle bruschetta with store-bought balsamic glaze just before serving.

VARIATION

To make a classic tomato bruschetta, simply replace the peach with diced vine-ripened tomatoes.

Baked Feta with Chile and Honey

This combination of salty feta, spicy chile and hot, sweet honey is hard to beat. You can prepare the dish beforehand, then pop it in the oven for 25 minutes and serve right away. The use of fresh and dried forms of chile together covers a wide spectrum of this spice's flavor profiles. Serve with crusty bread as an appetizer or as a side dish to a main course. Try it with Greek-Style Beef Stifado (page 88).

Makes 4 servings as a side or 6 as an appetizer

Preheat oven to 350°F (180°C)

8-inch (20 cm) glass baking dish, lightly greased

2 blocks (14 oz/400 g total) feta cheese, drained
3½ oz (105 g) cherry tomatoes, halved
1 fresh long red chile, finely diced
½ tsp Aleppo pepper flakes or mild pepper flakes
1 tsp lemon zest
1½ tbsp runny honey (see tip)
1 tbsp olive oil
½ tsp black sesame seeds, for garnish (optional)

1. Place feta blocks in the prepared glass baking dish. Scatter tomatoes around the cheese.
2. Evenly top with fresh and dried chiles and lemon zest.
3. Drizzle honey and oil evenly over feta and tomatoes.
4. Place in preheated oven and bake for 25 minutes, or until feta is golden and soft enough to spread on bread slices. Serve immediately, garnished with sesame seeds (if using).

TIPS

Be sure to use runny honey to achieve the right texture for drizzling over the feta.

No salt is needed, as feta is already very salty.

Simple Chile Lime Chicken Stir-Fry

This quick, tasty stir-fry combines tender chicken with the zesty freshness of lime and the heat of red chile. Serve with Roasted Allspice Sweet Potato (page 67) for a healthy midweek meal.

Makes 2 servings

1 lb (500 g) chicken breasts, cut into 1-inch (2.5 cm) cubes
1 long red chile, quartered lengthwise, then finely diced
1 large clove garlic, sliced
1 tbsp brown sugar
1 tsp lime zest
2 tbsp (30 mL) lime juice
1 tbsp vegetable oil
Salt and freshly ground black pepper

1. In a medium bowl, combine chicken, chile, garlic, brown sugar, lime zest, and lime juice. Stir to coat evenly, then let marinate for 15 minutes at room temperature (or place in an airtight container and marinate overnight in the refrigerator).
2. Heat oil in a large skillet over medium-high heat. Add chicken and marinade to the skillet. Cook, stirring continuously, until chicken is no longer pink inside, 7 to 8 minutes.
3. Season to taste with salt and pepper. Serve immediately.

VARIATION

For a more Asian-style stir-fry, replace vegetable oil with sesame oil, and add 1 tbsp of soy sauce to the marinade in step 1. Serve with steamed rice and Chinese greens.

Steak with Chimichurri Salsa

This flavorful steak is paired with a vibrant South American chimichurri sauce, featuring fresh parsley, cilantro and a good dose of heat from dried hot pepper flakes. Serve with Roasted Garlic White Bean Mash (page 106), or buttered rice.

Makes 2 servings

Food processor

Grill pan

CHIMICHURRI SALSA

- 1 cup (250 mL) roughly chopped parsley
- ½ cup (125 mL) roughly chopped cilantro
- 2 cloves garlic
- 1 tsp hot pepper flakes
- ½ tsp sea salt
- ⅓ cup (75 mL) olive oil
- 3 tbsp (45 mL) red wine vinegar

STEAK

- 2 (8 oz/250 g) sirloin steaks, at room temperature (see tip)
- ½ tsp salt
- ½ tsp freshly ground black pepper
- 1 tbsp butter

1. *Chimichurri Salsa:* In bowl of food processor, combine parsley, cilantro, garlic, hot pepper flakes, salt, oil and vinegar. Blitz until a rough paste forms.

2. *Steak:* Heat grill pan over high heat. Season both sides of steaks with salt and pepper.

3. Add butter to pan and cook steaks for 2 minutes on each side. Continue cooking for 4 minutes on each side for medium-rare.

4. Remove steaks from the pan and let rest for 2 minutes. Serve with a generous dollop of chimichurri salsa on top.

TIPS

Allowing steak to come to room temperature ensures more uniform cooking throughout. A cold steak will lower the heat of the pan, which will keep it from getting the ultimate seal and crust that comes from high heat.

Leftover chimichurri salsa can be refrigerated in an airtight container for up to 3 weeks or frozen for up to 3 months.

For a bolder sauce, let chimichurri sit for an hour before serving.

One-Bowl Chile Chocolate Brownie

Brownies are one of those universally popular recipes that can be made in no time and without any fuss. This version is infused with a touch of chile, complementing the richness of dark chocolate and taking it to new heights of deliciousness.

Makes 25 brownies

Preheat oven to 350°F (180°C)

8-inch (20 cm) square baking pan, greased and lined with parchment paper

8 oz (250 g) 70% bittersweet (dark) chocolate, broken into pieces

2/3 cup (150 mL) unsalted butter, cut into pieces

1 cup (250 mL) superfine (caster) sugar (see tip)

2 large eggs, lightly beaten

1 tsp pure vanilla extract

1/4 tsp ground mild chile (such as pasilla, ancho or Kashmiri)

2/3 cup (150 mL) all-purpose flour

1. In a heatproof bowl set over a saucepan of simmering water (or in a double boiler), combine chocolate and butter. Heat gently, stirring occasionally, until fully melted and smooth. Remove from heat and let cool slightly.

2. Stir sugar into melted chocolate mixture until fully incorporated. Add eggs, vanilla and ground chile and combine well.

3. Gradually fold in flour until batter is smooth (do not overmix).

4. Pour batter into prepared pan and smooth the top with a spatula.

5. Bake in preheated oven for 45 to 50 minutes, or until a skewer inserted in the center comes out with just a few moist crumbs.

6. Let brownies cool in the pan for 10 minutes before transferring to a wire rack. Once completely cool, cut into squares.

TIP

If you can't find superfine sugar, process granulated sugar in a food processor with the metal blade until it reaches a sand-like consistency.

VARIATION

For individual portions, pour batter into 24 paper-lined muffin cups, filling them halfway, and bake for 20 minutes.

Grilled Beef with Asian Slaw

This vibrant, healthy satisfying dish combines tender grilled beef with a crisp, refreshing slaw packed with fresh cilantro and a zesty dressing. The slaw is actually a great side salad for any barbecue, as it won't wilt quickly after being dressed.

Makes 4 servings

Blender or food processor

Grill or grill pan

TIPS

Julienning vegetables involves cutting them into very thin, matchstick-size pieces.

BEEF

12 oz (375 g) sirloin steak

1 tbsp sesame oil

Salt and freshly ground black pepper

DRESSING

1 long red chile pepper, seeded and roughly chopped

⅓ cup (75 mL) lime juice (from about 2 limes)

1 tbsp coconut sugar or granulated sugar

1 tbsp fish sauce

1 tsp sesame oil

SLAW

1 small carrot, cut into 4-inch (10 cm) julienne

½ large red bell pepper, julienned (see tip)

4½ cups (1.125 L) finely sliced napa cabbage

3 cups (750 mL) finely sliced red cabbage

¾ cup (175 mL) julienned lengthwise snow peas

1 cup (250 mL) loosely packed fresh cilantro leaves, roughly chopped

½ cup (125 mL) loosely packed fresh mint leaves, roughly chopped

6 green onions, finely sliced

2 tbsp (30 mL) sesame seeds

⅓ cup (75 mL) unsalted raw cashews or peanuts, roughly chopped

1. *Beef:* Rub sirloin steak with oil and season with salt and pepper.

2. *Dressing:* In blender or food processor, combine chile, lime juice, sugar, fish sauce and oil. Blend until smooth. Adjust seasoning to taste.

3. *Slaw:* In a large mixing bowl, combine carrot, red pepper, napa cabbage, red cabbage, snow peas, cilantro, mint, green onions, sesame seeds and cashews. Toss to combine evenly. Pour dressing over slaw and toss again to coat.

4. Heat grill or grill pan over high heat. Grill steak to your desired doneness: 3 to 4 minutes per side for medium-rare. Remove from the heat and let rest for 5 minutes before slicing thinly against the grain.

5. Divide slaw among serving plates and top with slices of grilled beef. Serve immediately.

Cilantro and Black Bean Salsa

This wonderful salsa is extremely versatile. Serve it as a side at barbecues or add some quinoa and lettuce for a stand-alone salad. Ideal for serving alongside Texas-Style Ribs (page 92).

Makes 4 servings

1 can (14 oz/398 mL) black beans, drained and rinsed

1 avocado, peeled and diced

1 tbsp finely chopped red onion

2 tbsp (30 mL) fresh lime juice

¼ cup (60 mL) loosely packed fresh cilantro leaves

½ tsp fine sea salt

Additional sea salt, if needed

1. In a bowl, stir together black beans, avocado, red onion, lime juice, cilantro and salt. Season with more salt to taste.

2. Keep refrigerated until ready to serve. This salsa will last for up to 3 days in an airtight container in the refrigerator.

VARIATIONS

For a chile kick, add 1 chopped green jalapeño pepper (with its seeds).

Replace black beans with kidney beans or use a combination of the two.

Pork Tenderloin in Orange Sauce

This dish highlights coriander seed as a subtle yet essential spice, perfectly complementing the sweet, tangy orange sauce, soy and caramelized onions for a well-rounded flavor profile.

Makes 6 servings

- Olive oil
- Zest and juice of 2 oranges
- 2 tbsp (30 mL) soy sauce
- 2 tbsp (30 mL) white wine vinegar
- 2 tbsp (30 mL) ground coriander
- 1 tsp fine sea salt
- 3 pork tenderloin fillets (about 8 oz/250 g each)
- 4 onions, halved and finely sliced
- $\frac{1}{4}$ cup (60 mL) granulated sugar
- $\frac{3}{4}$ cup (175 mL) dry sherry
- Additional sea salt
- Freshly ground black pepper

1. In a shallow bowl, combine 2 tbsp (30 mL) oil, orange zest and juice, soy sauce, vinegar, coriander and 1 tsp salt. Add pork, turning to coat. Cover and refrigerate for at least 1 hour.

2. Heat oil in a skillet over low heat. Add onions and sugar, stirring well to combine. Cover with a tight-fitting lid and cook, stirring occasionally, until soft, about 15 minutes. Remove the lid and cook, stirring often, until golden, 2 to 3 minutes.

3. Remove pork from marinade, letting any excess liquid drain back into the bowl. Reserve marinade. Heat oil in another skillet over medium heat. Add pork and cook, turning occasionally, until just a hint of pink remains, 8 to 12 minutes. Transfer to a plate and cover with foil to keep warm.

4. In the same skillet, bring reserved marinade to a boil over medium heat. Cook, stirring occasionally, until reduced to a thick syrup, about 10 minutes. Add sherry and return to a boil. Season with salt and pepper to taste.

5. Slice pork diagonally into 1-inch (2.5 cm) pieces. Divide among six plates, top with caramelized onions and drizzle with orange sauce.

TIP

Cooking the onions slowly is key to achieving a rich, caramelized flavor.

Apple and Pear Cobbler

Cobblers are a great dessert with minimal effort and delicious results. The fruit can be varied according to what's in season, but the combination of warming spices makes cobblers ideal for the cooler months.

Makes 6 servings

Preheat oven to 375°F (190°C)

9-inch (23 cm) round or square baking dish, greased

FILLING

1½ lbs (750 g) pears, peeled, cored and sliced

12 oz (375 g) apples, peeled, cored and sliced

2 tbsp (30 mL) granulated sugar

1 tsp ground coriander

¼ tsp ground cinnamon

1 tbsp lemon juice

TOPPING

1 cup (250 mL) all-purpose flour

3 tbsp (45 mL) quick-cooking rolled oats

2 tbsp (30 mL) granulated sugar

½ tsp ground coriander

½ tsp baking powder

1¼ cups (310 mL) heavy or whipping (35%) cream

1. *Filling:* In a large mixing bowl, combine sliced pears and apples with sugar, coriander, cinnamon and lemon juice. Toss well to coat. Transfer mixture to prepared baking dish and spread into an even layer.

2. *Topping:* In another large bowl, whisk together flour, rolled oats, sugar, coriander and baking powder. Gradually pour in cream, stirring until just combined. The mixture should be slightly sticky.

3. Spoon dollops of topping mixture over filling, spreading gently to cover most of the fruit while leaving some gaps for steam to escape.

4. Bake in preheated oven for 40 to 45 minutes, or until topping is golden brown and filling is bubbling.

5. Let cobbler cool for 10 minutes before serving.

TIPS

The cobbler can be prepared a day ahead, or frozen before cooking. Add 20 minutes to the baking time or bring to room temperature before baking.

Leftovers can be stored in the refrigerator for up to 3 days and reheated gently before serving.

The Best Banana Muffins

The keys to great banana muffins are very ripe (think: black skin) bananas and, of course, the unmistakable flavor of cinnamon. Just when you think your bananas are ready for the trash, they are actually at their best for baking, with a soft texture and concentrated natural sugars.

Makes 12 muffins

Preheat oven to 350°F (180°C)

12-cup muffin pan, lined with large baking cups

2 cups (500 mL) self-rising flour
¾ cup (175 mL) light brown sugar
2 tsp ground cinnamon
1 tsp baking powder
2 large eggs, lightly whisked
½ cup (125 mL) butter, melted and cooled
½ cup (125 mL) milk
3 very ripe bananas (about 1 lb/500 g)

1. In a large bowl, combine flour, brown sugar, cinnamon and baking powder.
2. In a medium bowl, combine eggs, butter and milk.
3. In a separate bowl, mash bananas well, then add to the milk mixture, mixing with a large whisk.
4. Add banana mixture to dry ingredients, stirring gently with a metal spoon until just combined. Be careful not to overmix.
5. Divide batter equally among prepared muffin cups. Bake in preheated oven for 25 minutes or until risen and golden on top. When lightly pressed, muffins should spring back without leaving a dent.
6. Remove muffin pan from oven and let muffins cool in pan for 5 minutes. Transfer to a wire rack to cool completely.

TIPS

Make a cinnamon-sugar mix (1:2 ratio) to sprinkle on top of the warm muffins after baking for added flavor.

Once completely cooled, muffins can be placed in an airtight container and frozen for up to 3 months.

Greek-Style Beef Stifado

This fragrant, comforting Greek stew combines tender beef, pearl onions and a robust blend of herbs and spices. Serve with mashed potatoes, rice or orzo pasta for a hearty, satisfying meal.

Makes 6 servings

Preheat oven to 300°F (150°C)

Dutch oven with lid

2 lbs (1 kg) stewing beef, cut into 3-inch pieces
14 oz (400 g) pearl onions, peeled
4 large cloves garlic, sliced
2 fresh or dried bay leaves
1 sprig fresh rosemary
1 tbsp dried oregano
½ tsp ground cinnamon
⅓ cup (75 mL) dry red wine
1 tbsp (15 mL) red wine vinegar
1 can (14 oz/398 mL) crushed tomatoes
Salt and freshly ground black pepper
Water, as needed

1. To a sealable bag, add beef, pearl onions, garlic, bay leaves, rosemary, oregano, cinnamon, red wine and vinegar. Seal bag, massage to coat and refrigerate for 2 to 24 hours, turning occasionally to coat beef evenly.

2. Heat Dutch oven over high heat. Remove beef from marinade (reserve marinade) and brown it in Dutch oven for about 5 minutes (see tip).

3. Reduce heat to low. Add reserved marinade, tomatoes and enough water to just cover beef. Season with salt and pepper, then stir to combine.

4. Bring mixture to a gentle simmer on the stovetop, then cover Dutch oven with lid and transfer to middle rack of preheated oven. Cook for 2 hours. Remove lid for stew sauce to thicken and cook until meat is tender and falling apart, about 30 minutes.

Tips

The wet marinade will prevent deep browning.

Leftovers can be stored in the refrigerator for up to 3 days or frozen in an airtight container for up to 3 months.

Quick Chickpea Curry

This is a quick, easy vegan curry, and a great example of how sweet cinnamon combines with earthy spices to create a balanced, delicious result. Serve with Baked Basmati Rice Pilaf (page 91) or as part of a bigger Indian meal.

Makes 4 side servings

1 tbsp coconut oil
1 onion, minced
3 cloves garlic, minced
1 tsp ground coriander
1 tsp ground cumin
½ tsp ground turmeric
½ tsp ground cinnamon
¼ tsp cayenne pepper
¼ tsp paprika
¼ tsp fine sea salt
2 cups (500 mL) cooked chickpeas
1 cup (250 mL) crushed tomatoes with juice
1 cup (250 mL) water
½ cup (125 mL) coconut yogurt (or Greek yogurt)
Additional sea salt
Freshly ground black pepper

1. In a large saucepan, melt coconut oil over medium heat. Add onion and garlic, and sauté until softened, about 3 minutes.
2. Add coriander, cumin, turmeric, cinnamon, cayenne, paprika and ¼ tsp salt. Stir and cook, until spices are fragrant and well combined, about 2 minutes.
3. Stir in chickpeas, tomatoes and 1 cup (250 mL) water. Combine well. Reduce heat and simmer, stirring occasionally, until curry is thickened, about 15 minutes.
4. Stir through yogurt and season to taste with additional salt and pepper.

TIP

Garnish with fresh cilantro and a squeeze of lime juice for an extra burst of flavor.

Baked Basmati Rice Pilaf

This beautiful, flavorful rice dish is a perfect choice for entertaining and can be served straight from the oven. The fragrance from the whole cinnamon penetrates the rice, and the sticks can be removed just before serving.

Makes 6 to 8 servings

Preheat oven to 425°F (220°C)

2½ cups (625 mL) white or brown basmati rice, soaked for 1 to 3 hours, rinsed and drained

2 whole cinnamon sticks, broken in half

1 tsp sea salt

2 tbsp (30 mL) butter, cut into ½-inch (1 cm) cubes

4 cups (1 L) boiling ready-to-use vegetable or chicken broth

1. Transfer drained rinsed rice to baking dish. Sprinkle cinnamon sticks and salt evenly over rice, then dot top with butter cubes.

2. Pour boiling broth over rice. Cover dish tightly with foil and bake in preheated oven for 20 minutes.

3. Remove dish from oven and let it rest for 10 minutes without removing foil. Remove the cinnamon sticks before serving.

TIP

Serve with a generous amount of fresh cilantro and flaked almonds, if desired.

VARIATION

Add a pinch of dried saffron to broth before pouring it over rice in step 2, for added flavor and color.

Texas-Style Ribs

With their spiced sweet-and-sour marinade, these delicious ribs will disappear in no time. They are easy to prepare a day ahead by slow-roasting, and finished off on the barbecue the next day. Serve with Cilantro and Black Bean Salsa (page 82).

Makes 4 servings

Preheat oven to 300°F (150°C)

Baking sheet, lined with foil

- 2 tbsp (30 mL) garlic powder
- 1 tbsp ground cumin
- 1½ tsp paprika
- 1 tsp ground cinnamon
- 1 tsp cayenne pepper
- ½ tsp ground allspice
- ½ tsp salt
- ½ tsp freshly ground black pepper
- ½ cup (125 mL) ketchup
- ¼ cup (60 mL) cider vinegar
- ¼ cup (60 mL) apple juice
- 2 tbsp (30 mL) pure maple syrup
- 1 tbsp soy sauce
- 1 tbsp brown sugar
- 2.6 lbs (1.2 kg) rack pork ribs, silverskin removed (see tip)

1. In a small saucepan over low heat, combine garlic powder, cumin, paprika, cinnamon, cayenne, allspice, salt, black pepper, ketchup, vinegar, apple juice, maple syrup, soy sauce and brown sugar. Heat gently, stirring occasionally, until sugar has dissolved. Remove from heat and let cool.
2. Place ribs in a large plastic bag or shallow dish. Pour marinade over ribs, ensuring they are evenly coated. Seal bag or cover dish and refrigerate for 2 to 24 hours to let the flavors develop.
3. Place marinated ribs on prepared baking sheet and cover with foil, reserving any leftover marinade. Bake in preheated oven for 2 hours, turning ribs once halfway through cooking and basting with marinade. When done, the meat should be very tender.
4. To finish, preheat a hot grill and cook ribs for 5 minutes on each side, or until caramelized. Alternatively, turn the oven to broil and cook for 5 minutes on each side or bake at 400°F (200°C) for 10 minutes.

TIPS

Prepare an extra portion of marinade and freeze in an airtight container for up to 6 months.

Silverskin is a tough piece of membrane that is sometimes on the bone side of pork ribs. If it's not removed before cooking, it can prevent the ribs from absorbing the seasonings and the meat can become chewy. To remove, use a small sharp knife to cut along the edge of the silverskin until there is enough to hold onto, then pull the silverskin off in one piece.

Xinjiang Chicken Stir-Fry

As always, the origin of a dish is a fascinating insight into history, in which spices play a huge part. The Xinjiang region in China is predominantly made up of citizens of Uyghur heritage, making the heavy use of cumin extremely natural even though it's not typically associated with Chinese cuisine. This chicken stir-fry, perfect served with steamed jasmine rice, has a unique and pleasing flavor.

Makes 4 servings

Wok or deep skillet

1½ lbs (750 g) boneless chicken thighs, cut into strips
2 tsp minced garlic
2 tsp minced fresh gingerroot
2 tsp cumin seeds, divided (see tip)
2 tbsp (30 mL) sesame oil
2 tbsp (30 mL) vegetable oil
3 yellow onions, cut into wedges
1 large red bell pepper, cut into 1-inch (2.5 cm) pieces
½ tsp ground Szechuan pepper (or cayenne pepper)
2 tbsp (30 mL) rice wine vinegar
1 long red chile pepper, sliced
1 cup (250 mL) loosely packed fresh cilantro, chopped
1 tbsp toasted sesame seeds

1. In a medium bowl, combine chicken with garlic, ginger and 1 tsp cumin seeds. Cover and marinate for 30 minutes, or refrigerate overnight for more intense flavor.
2. Heat oils in wok over medium-high heat. Add onions and red pepper and stir-fry for 3 minutes, or until slightly softened.
3. Add marinated chicken, remaining cumin seeds, Szechuan pepper and vinegar. Stir-fry until chicken is cooked through and juices run clear when pierced, 6 to 8 minutes.
4. Top stir-fry with chile pepper, cilantro and sesame seeds.

TIP

For added depth of flavor, toast cumin seeds in a small dry skillet over low heat for 2 minutes, until fragrance is released. Remove from pan immediately to prevent burning.

Artichoke Dip

The fresh flavor of artichokes paired with earthy cumin makes this a mouthwatering dip that is best served warm with crusty bread.

Makes 2 servings

Food processor (or blender)

1 to 2 tbsp (15 to 30 mL) olive oil

6 black olives, pitted and chopped

1 can (15 oz/425 g) artichoke hearts, drained and roughly chopped

1 small tomato, roughly chopped

1 small clove garlic, chopped

2 tsp ground cumin

1 tsp ground mild chile, or to taste

Salt and freshly ground black pepper

Water, if needed

1 tbsp lemon juice

1. Heat oil in a skillet over medium heat. Add olives, artichokes, tomato, garlic, cumin, ground chile, and a pinch each of salt and pepper. Cook, stirring often, until tomato is softened and ingredients are heated through, 6 to 8 minutes. If mixture is too dry, add a small amount of water to combine.

2. Once tomato has softened, add lemon juice and season to taste with more salt and pepper. Process mixture in food processor to create a purée (see tip).

TIP

Keep the style of the dip rustic by skipping the purée step.

Couscous with Cumin-Spiced Roasted Vegetables

This hearty, aromatic dish combines roasted vegetables with fragrant cumin, served over fluffy couscous. Perfect as a vegetarian main or a side dish, it's a fantastic way to showcase seasonal produce. Serve alongside Midweek Meat Loaf (page 100) or Pork Tenderloin in Orange Sauce (page 83).

Makes 4 servings or 6 as a side dish

Preheat oven to 400°F (200°C)

- 1 red bell pepper, cut into 1½-inch (4 cm) pieces
- 1 lb (500 g) pumpkin, peeled and cut into 1½-inch (4 cm) pieces
- 12 oz (375 g) parsnips, peeled and quartered lengthwise, then cut in half
- 6 oz (175 g) small pickling onions, halved
- 1 tbsp ground cumin
- ¼ cup (60 mL) olive oil, divided
- 12 oz (375 g) zucchini, cut into chunks
- 1 cup (250 mL) uncooked couscous
- Salt and freshly ground black pepper, to taste
- 1 cup (250 mL) ready-to-use vegetable broth

1. Place red pepper, pumpkin, parsnips and onions on a baking sheet. Toss with cumin and 2 tbsp (30 mL) oil.
2. Bake in preheated oven for 15 minutes. Add zucchini, tossing in with other vegetables, and roast for 25 minutes, or until tender.
3. Place couscous in a large heatproof bowl; drizzle remaining oil over it and add a pinch of salt and pepper.
4. In a small saucepan over high heat, bring broth to a boil, then pour on top of couscous. Cover with plastic wrap or a plate to ensure no steam escapes. Let it sit for 5 minutes; fluff with a fork. Taste and adjust seasoning as needed.
5. Place couscous in a serving dish and top with roasted vegetables.

VARIATIONS

Substitute sweet potato or carrots for parsnips, if preferred.

Top with crumbled feta cheese before serving.

Orange, Fennel and Arugula Salad

This vibrant, attractive salad pairs the sweet juiciness of oranges with the crisp, anise-like flavor of shaved fennel and the peppery bite of arugula. This recipe uses fresh fennel and also fennel seeds, showcasing the plant's breadth of flavor. A refreshing side to serve with roast pork or as part of an Italian feast.

Makes 4 servings

Mandoline

1 tsp fennel seeds

1½ tbsp olive oil

1 tbsp lemon juice

¼ tsp salt

2 oz (60 g) arugula

2 oranges, segmented (see tip)

1 fresh fennel bulb, shaved finely with a mandoline (see tip)

¼ cup (60 mL) roughly chopped flat-leaf (Italian) parsley

1. Lightly crush fennel seeds with a mortar and pestle or the back of a spoon. In a small bowl, whisk together oil, lemon juice, fennel seeds and salt.

2. In a large bowl, combine arugula, oranges, fresh fennel shavings and parsley. Drizzle with dressing and gently toss to coat before serving.

TIPS

To segment an orange, cut off the top and bottom, then remove the peel and pith with a sharp knife. Slice between the membranes to release the segments.

A mandoline is a kitchen utensil for shaving vegetables thinly.

This dressing also makes a wonderful sauce for chilled seafood.

VARIATIONS

If in season, use blood oranges instead of regular oranges for an even prettier salad.

Top with torn buffalo mozzarella cheese.

Midweek Meat Loaf

Not only is meat loaf a family favorite, but it is great for preparing ahead. Our flavorful meat loaf recipe combines the aromatic essence of fennel with a touch of paprika's smoky depth. A perfect accompaniment to this dish is Couscous with Cumin-Spiced Roasted Vegetables (page 96). Of course, meat loaf leftovers are delicious cold, so they're perfect as a sandwich filling.

Makes 4 servings

Preheat oven to 400°F (200°C)

8- by 4-inch (20 by 10 cm) loaf pan, lined with parchment paper

---

1 onion, grated

1 lb (500 g) ground pork

8 oz (250 g) bacon, finely chopped

¼ cup (60 mL) dried bread crumbs

2 tsp ground fennel seeds

1 tsp smoked sweet paprika

½ tsp freshly ground black pepper

1 large egg

¼ cup (60 mL) milk

1. In a large bowl, combine onion, pork, bacon, bread crumbs, ground fennel, paprika and pepper. Use clean hands to combine thoroughly.

2. In a small bowl, whisk egg and milk together with a fork. Add this mixture to meat mixture and combine thoroughly with the fork or your hands, ensuring the ingredients are evenly distributed.

3. Press mixture into prepared loaf pan. Bake in preheated oven for 60 minutes or until cooked through, no longer pink inside and a meat thermometer inserted into the center reads 160°F (71°C).

4. Let cool in pan on a wire rack for 10 minutes. Using a spatula, transfer meat loaf to a serving dish and spoon any juices over the top.

TIP

This meat loaf can be prepared up to a day in advance. Cover and refrigerate until ready to bake, or freeze for up to 1 month.

VARIATION

Glaze with 2 tbsp (30 mL) of ketchup before baking.

Speedy Sausage and Fennel Penne

Pull this tasty dish together in less than 15 minutes. By using quality sausages (from a farmers' market or butcher, without unnecessary fillers), there is no need for onion, garlic or other regular pasta sauce ingredients. As fennel is the perfect partner to pork, it helps elevate this simple meal.

Makes 2 servings

9 oz (275 g) dried penne

10 oz (300 g) quality pork sausages

16 cherry tomatoes, halved

1 tsp whole fennel seeds, lightly bruised (see tip)

⅔ cup (150 mL) light (5%) cream

Salt and freshly ground black pepper

1. Bring a large pot of salted water to a boil (see tip). Add penne and cook according to package instructions.
2. While the pasta cooks, heat a large skillet over medium heat. Squeeze sausage meat from casings into skillet and discard casings. Use a wooden spoon to break sausage into small pieces as it browns, about 3 to 4 minutes.
3. Add tomatoes, fennel seeds and cream. Reduce heat to low and simmer for 5 minutes while the pasta finishes cooking.
4. Drain pasta (do not rinse under water) and return to the pot. Stir sausage sauce into cooked pasta until evenly coated.
5. Season to taste with salt and pepper and serve immediately.

TIPS

For perfectly salted pasta water, add 1 tbsp salt for every 4 cups (1 L) water.

To bruise fennel seeds, simply press with the back of a spoon; this releases the flavor.

VARIATION

Shred leftover rotisserie chicken and use in place of sausage.

Quick-Pickled Cucumber

This tangy pickled cucumber is perfect as a quick, refreshing side dish, a topping for sandwiches or an accompaniment to grilled meats. The anise flavor from fennel seeds gives this quick pickle a unique but versatile flavor.

Makes about 1 cup (250 mL)

1 long cucumber, 12 oz (375 g), seeded and cut into batons or slices (or a combination of both)

1 tbsp palm sugar or granulated sugar

1 tsp salt

1 tsp whole fennel seeds

2 tbsp (30 mL) white wine vinegar

1. In a shallow container with a lid, stir together cucumber, sugar, salt, fennel seeds and vinegar until cucumber is well coated.

2. Cover container with lid and marinate for at least 30 minutes, shaking container every 10 minutes.

TIP

These pickled cucumbers can be stored in an airtight container in the refrigerator for up to 5 days, during which time the flavor will intensify.

VARIATION

For added heat, include a pinch of hot pepper flakes or a thinly sliced red chile pepper.

Dough Balls with Garlic Butter

These soft, fluffy dough balls are an easy treat to make at home. Serve them fresh from the oven, with garlic butter melting on top.

Makes about 12 dough balls

Baking sheet, lined with parchment

1 cup (250 mL) bread flour

1 tsp granulated sugar

1 tsp quick-rising (instant) yeast

½ cup + 2 tbsp (155 mL) warm water (see tip)

1 tbsp olive oil

Pinch salt

3 tbsp (45 mL) unsalted butter, softened

2 cloves garlic, minced

2 tsp very finely chopped fresh parsley

1. In a large bowl, combine flour, sugar and yeast. Gradually mix in ½ cup + 2 tbsp (155 mL) water and oil until a soft dough forms. Add salt, and knead dough for about 8 minutes on a lightly floured surface until smooth and elastic (see tip).
2. Place dough in a large greased bowl, cover with plastic wrap and let it rise in a warm place for 1 hour, or until it has doubled in size.
3. Preheat oven to 400°F (200°C). Punch down the dough and divide it into 12 equal pieces. Roll each piece into a small ball and arrange on prepared baking sheet, leaving space between each ball. Cover and let rise for 20 minutes.
4. Bake dough balls for 10 to 12 minutes, or until lightly golden and cooked through.
5. While dough balls are baking, in a small bowl, combine butter, garlic and parsley.
6. Remove dough balls from oven and brush them generously with garlic butter. Serve warm.

TIPS

To activate yeast, the water needs to be warm, not boiling.

Dough is elastic when you push an indent into the dough and it springs back.

To freeze dough balls, let cool without brushing with garlic butter, then freeze in a freezer bag.

Garlic butter can also be frozen – it's fantastic melted on grilled steak.

Roasted Garlic White Bean Mash

Having roasted garlic on hand is an easy way to add soft and sweet garlic flavor to any dish (it's even great for small children or people with a sensitivity to garlic). Roasted garlic shines in this creamy white bean mash that is a delicious alternative to mashed potatoes.

Makes 4 servings

Preheat oven to 400°F (200°C)

TIP

Roast multiple bulbs of garlic at the same time, then store the cloves in a jar, covered with olive oil, in the refrigerator for up to 1 month.

1 whole garlic bulb

Olive oil

2 tbsp (30 mL) unsalted butter or olive oil

2 cans (14 oz/398 mL each) cannellini (white kidney) beans, drained and rinsed

½ cup (125 mL) ready-to-use vegetable or chicken broth, plus more as needed

Salt and freshly ground black pepper, to taste

Fresh parsley, for garnish (optional)

1. Place garlic in foil, drizzle 1 tbsp oil over top and wrap foil to seal.
2. Roast in preheated oven for 30 to 35 minutes, or until garlic is soft and caramelized. Let cool slightly, then squeeze the roasted cloves out of the skins.
3. Melt the butter in a medium saucepan over low heat; add beans and broth. Heat gently, stirring occasionally, until warmed through.
4. Add roasted garlic to beans. Using a potato masher, mash beans mixture until smooth and creamy, adding more broth if necessary to reach your desired consistency (see tip).
5. Season to taste with salt and pepper. Transfer to a serving dish, drizzle with oil, and garnish with parsley if desired.

TIP

For a smoother texture, use a food processor or immersion blender. For a rustic, chunkier mash, a potato masher works well.

VARIATION

Stir in 2 tbsp (30 mL) of grated Parmesan cheese in step 5 for added richness.

Chile Garlic Oil

This versatile chile garlic oil is a delicious condiment that is perfect for drizzling over noodles, pizzas and grilled dishes, or for bottling and gifting to friends.

Makes about 1½ cups (375 mL)

1 cup (250 mL) olive oil

½ cup (125 mL) neutral-flavored oil, such as rice bran or vegetable oil

6 whole dried red chiles

4 cloves garlic, peeled and bruised

1 tsp hot pepper flakes

1. In a small saucepan over low heat, combine olive oil, neutral oil, whole dried chiles, garlic and hot pepper flakes. Heat gently for about 10 minutes, or until small bubbles rise to the surface and the oil is fragrant. Do not let the oil boil or the chiles and garlic will burn.

2. Remove the saucepan from the heat and let cool completely for 2 hours while flavors infuse.

3. Discard the garlic. Using a funnel, pour the oil, along with the whole chiles and hot pepper flakes, into a sterilized jar or bottle (see tip).

4. The chile oil can be used immediately, but the flavor will mature over time. Store in a cool, dark place for up to 1 year.

TIP

To sterilize the jar, clean it thoroughly in hot soapy water, then drip-dry. Place the jar, right side up, on a baking sheet and heat in a preheated 400°F (200°C) oven for 10 minutes. To sterilize the lid, place it in a saucepan, cover with water and boil for 5 minutes. Handle lids and jars with clean hands.

VARIATION

Add a pinch of ground Szechuan peppercorns in step 1 for a numbing touch.

Cajun Blackened Garlic Shrimp

Cajun seasoning is a medium-heat blend that suits seafood perfectly when cooked in foaming garlic butter. Serve this shrimp on a bed of fresh green salad leaves for a light and tasty starter.

Makes 4 servings

CAJUN SPICE MIX

1 tbsp mild paprika

1 tbsp dried basil

1 tsp freshly ground black pepper

1 tsp garlic powder

1 tsp salt

½ tsp ground cinnamon

½ tsp ground fennel seed

½ tsp dried thyme

½ tsp cayenne pepper

SHRIMP

1 lb (500 g) large shrimp, peeled and deveined

2 tbsp (30 mL) butter

1 large clove garlic, crushed

1. *Cajun Spice Mix:* In a medium bowl, stir together paprika, basil, black pepper, garlic powder, salt, cinnamon, fennel seed, thyme and cayenne pepper.

2. *Shrimp:* Pat shrimp dry with a paper towel. Toss shrimp in spice mix to coat evenly.

3. Heat butter in a large skillet over medium-high heat. When butter is foaming and starting to turn darker, add garlic and sauté until fragrant, about 1 minute.

4. Add shrimp and cook, stirring, until opaque and cooked through, about 3 to 4 minutes; serve immediately.

TIPS

The key to achieving the signature blackened crust is to let the butter to start "burning," reaching the foaming stage, before adding shrimp.

VARIATION

For a Creole-style dish, deglaze pan with ¼ cup (60 mL) light (5%) cream and 2 tbsp (30 mL) tomato paste after cooking shrimp, then drizzle this sauce over the top before serving.

Kale and Quinoa Salad with Ginger Dressing

This hearty, nutritious salad combines kale, crunchy nuts and sweet pomegranate seeds with a bright ginger dressing. It's perfect as a main meal with grilled chicken or Cauliflower Popcorn (page 148) or as a satisfying side dish.

Makes 2 servings or 4 as a side dish

- 1½ oz (45 g) raw almonds, halved
- 1 oz (30 g) raw green pumpkin seeds
- ½ tsp tamari or soy sauce
- ¾ tsp sea salt, divided
- ¼ tsp Aleppo pepper flakes
- 3 tbsp (45 mL) apple cider vinegar
- 3 tbsp (45 mL) extra virgin olive oil
- 2 tsp grated fresh gingerroot
- 1 tsp runny honey
- 5 oz (150 g) raw kale, chopped into 1-inch (2.5 cm) pieces, thick veins removed
- 3½ oz (105 g) red or white quinoa, cooked and thoroughly drained
- ¼ cup (60 mL) pomegranate seeds

1. In a dry small skillet over medium heat, combine almonds, pumpkin seeds, tamari, ¼ tsp sea salt and pepper flakes. Toast, stirring frequently, until pumpkin seeds begin to pop, about 2 to 3 minutes. Remove from pan immediately to prevent burning.

2. In a small jar or small bowl, combine vinegar, oil, ginger, honey and ½ tsp salt. Shake well or whisk together to emulsify.

3. Place kale in a large bowl. Pour half the dressing over kale and massage with your hands for 1 to 2 minutes to soften the leaves.

4. Add quinoa and nuts mixture to the kale. Drizzle with remaining dressing and toss gently to combine. Top with pomegranate seeds.

TIP

Toasted nuts and seeds are a super-healthy salad topper to have on hand. Once completely cool, store in an airtight jar in the cupboard for up to 3 weeks.

Crisp Stovetop Ginger Granola

This is a scrumptious weekend breakfast if you don't have granola handy. Quickly making this on the stovetop and serving it warm with thick Greek yogurt is an unbeatable way to start your day. The ground ginger gives this granola lovely depth and warmth alongside the sweetness of the cinnamon, maple syrup and raisins.

Makes 1½ cups (375 mL) granola

- 2 tbsp (30 mL) olive oil
- 1 cup (250 mL) quick-cooking rolled oats
- 1 tsp ground ginger
- ¼ tsp ground cinnamon
- 2 tbsp (30 mL) raw green pumpkin seeds
- 2 tbsp (30 mL) roughly chopped pistachios
- 3 tbsp (45 mL) pure maple syrup
- 2 tbsp (30 mL) raisins

1. In a large skillet, heat oil over medium heat. Add oats, ginger and cinnamon. Stirring frequently, cook until oats are golden and spices are fragrant, about 3 to 4 minutes.

2. Stir in pumpkin seeds and pistachios. Cook, stirring often, until lightly toasted, about 2 minutes. Drizzle maple syrup evenly over oats mixture, stirring to coat. Cook until granola becomes crisp, about 1 to 2 minutes. Remove from heat and stir in raisins.

3. Serve immediately or store in an airtight container at room temperature for up to 1 week.

TIPS

Add a pinch of sea salt for a savory-sweet balance.

Do not add raisins until after granola has been removed from heat, as they will become too dry.

VARIATION

Swap raisins for dried cranberries or chopped apricots for variety.

Chicken and Olive Tagine

This warming, hearty Moroccan stew combines tender chicken with chickpeas and mild spices for a comforting family-friendly dish. Serve with fluffy, salted couscous and fresh cilantro for an authentic meal experience.

Makes 6 servings

Dutch oven

TIP

Preserved lemons differ from standard lemons in that the skin is soft and edible. If preserved ones are unavailable, add 2 tbsp (30 mL) lemon juice.

GINGER SPICE BLEND

2 tsp ground ginger
1 tsp ground cumin
1 tsp ground coriander
1 tsp sweet paprika
½ tsp ground cinnamon
½ tsp ground turmeric

TAGINE

2 tbsp (30 mL) olive oil
2 lbs (1 kg) boneless skinless chicken thighs, cut into 2-inch (5 cm) pieces
3 carrots, peeled and cut into ¾-inch (2 cm) pieces
2 cans chickpeas (each 14 to 19 oz/398 to 540 mL), drained and rinsed
1 can (28 oz/796 mL) diced tomatoes
1 preserved lemon, rind only, finely chopped (see tip)
2 tbsp (30 mL) Ginger Spice Blend, at left
2 cups (500 mL) loosely packed fresh spinach
1 cup (250 mL) large, firm green olives
Salt and freshly ground black pepper

1. *Ginger Spice Blend:* In a small bowl, stir together ginger, cumin, coriander, paprika, cinnamon and turmeric until well combined.
2. *Tagine:* In Dutch oven, heat oil over medium-high heat. Add chicken pieces and brown on all sides, about 5 minutes.
3. Add carrots, chickpeas, tomatoes, lemon and Ginger Spice Blend. Stir to combine.
4. Reduce heat to medium-low and let simmer, stirring occasionally, until carrots are tender and chicken is cooked through (no longer pink inside), about 20 minutes.
5. Stir in spinach and olives. Cook until spinach wilts and olives are heated through, about 5 minutes.
6. Season to taste with salt and pepper.

TIPS

The Ginger Spice Blend also complements roasted pumpkin or squash nicely.

Soy and Ginger Steamed Seabass

This dish is an excellent example of simplicity of flavors. By steaming the ginger with the fish, it becomes soft and pleasant to eat, with the sharpness dialed down by cooking. Serve with fluffy jasmine rice to make a complete meal.

Makes 2 servings

Bamboo steamer with lid, lined with parchment paper

10 oz (300 g) seabass fillets

½ oz (15 g) fresh gingerroot, peeled and cut into matchsticks

3 green onions, white parts only, cut into matchsticks

1 long red chile, sliced

1 tbsp sesame oil

2 tbsp (30 mL) soy sauce

3 pieces baby bok choy

1. Place fish in the lined steamer and top with ginger, green onions, chile slices, sesame oil, soy sauce and baby bok choy.
2. Fill a deep, wide saucepan with just enough water to ensure that the bottom of the steamer will not touch the water when placed into the pan. Bring to a boil over high heat.
3. Place the steamer with lid into the pan. Lower heat to maintain a simmer.
4. Cook until fish is opaque and bok choy is tender, about 8 minutes.
5. Serve immediately from steamer.

TIPS

For a gluten-free diet, replace the soy sauce with gluten-free tamari.

Bamboo steamers are widely available at Asian stores. A metal steamer can also be used.

VARIATION

Any flaky white fish can be used, as well as salmon fillets.

Lamb Burgers with Mint Yogurt Sauce

This recipe makes for a refreshing change from traditional beef burgers. The dried mint gives a subtle taste to the burger, and fresh mint elevates the yogurt sauce.

Makes 4 servings

12 oz (375 g) ground lamb

2 tsp dried mint

Salt and freshly ground black pepper

1 cup (250 mL) plain yogurt

¼ cup (60 mL) finely chopped fresh mint leaves

4 burger buns, lightly toasted

2 tomatoes, cut into slices

½ cucumber, cut into slices

½ red onion, finely sliced

1. In a large bowl, combine lamb, dried mint, ½ tsp salt and ½ tsp pepper. Combine gently but thoroughly.

2. Divide mixture into 4 equal portions and shape into burger patties.

3. Heat a barbecue or grill pan over medium-high heat. Cook patties until browned, about 3 to 4 minutes per side, or until cooked to your desired doneness.

4. In a small bowl, combine yogurt and fresh mint and season with salt and pepper to taste. Stir well.

5. Spread a generous amount of mint yogurt sauce on bottom half of each burger bun. Add a lamb patty, then top with tomato, cucumber and red onion. Finish each with top half of the bun.

TIP

Once shaped, the raw burgers can be wrapped tightly in plastic wrap and frozen for up to 3 months. Thaw before cooking as above.

Virgin Mojito

The combination of mint, sugar and lime in the form of a drink began in sixteenth century Havana and, by the nineteenth century, the addition of rum turned it into one of the most popular cocktails in the world. You can enjoy our version, with or without rum, for a refreshing and delicious beverage that lets mint take center stage.

Makes 6 servings

3 large juicy limes, cut into wedges

1 cup (250 mL) packed fresh mint leaves (about 30 to 40 leaves)

½ cup (125 mL) granulated sugar

3 cups (750 mL) ice cubes

6 cups (1.5 L) soda or sparkling water

Extra mint sprigs and lime slices, for garnish

1. In a large bowl, combine lime, mint and sugar.
2. Use a muddler or a wooden spoon to gently but thoroughly crush the ingredients, releasing the lime juice and mint oils and dissolving the sugar.
3. Evenly distribute lime mixture among six tall glasses. Divide ice among glasses and top with soda water.
4. Serve each with extra mint and lime and a straw, if desired.

TIP

Transform these mocktails into cocktails by adding 9 oz (270 mL) white rum at the end of step 2.

Pea and Mint Hummus

This twist on traditional hummus is a wonderful dip to enjoy in the spring, with its vibrant green color and burst of minty flavor. Serve it with breadsticks and crudités or alongside grilled lamb.

Makes 1½ cups (375 mL)

Food processor

1 can (14 oz/398 mL) chickpeas, drained and rinsed
1 cup (250 mL) frozen peas, thawed
2 sprigs mint, stemmed
1 clove garlic, crushed
¼ cup (60 mL) extra virgin olive oil
¼ cup (60 mL) lemon juice
1 tbsp tahini
Salt
Additional lemon juice, if needed

1. In food processor, combine chickpeas, peas, mint leaves, garlic, oil, lemon juice, tahini and 1 tsp salt. Blend for 3 to 4 minutes, until smooth and creamy.
2. If hummus is too thick, add 1 to 2 tbsp (15 to 30 mL) water and blend again until desired consistency is reached.
3. Taste; adjust seasoning if needed by adding more lemon juice or salt.

TIP

Drizzle with extra olive oil and garnish with a few mint leaves or a sprinkle of lemon zest before serving.

VARIATION

For a winter hummus, replace peas with cooked beetroot, and mint with 1 tsp ground cumin.

Watermelon, Haloumi and Mint Salad

It's incredible how delicious the combination of just a few simple ingredients can be. In this recipe, juicy, sweet watermelon, salty haloumi and refreshing mint are tied together with a little oil and vinegar to create a wonderfully tasty salad to serve on a hot day.

Makes 4 servings

14 oz (400 g) ripe watermelon, seeds removed, cut into 3-inch (7.5 cm) triangles

1 tbsp white balsamic (or regular balsamic) vinegar

8 oz (250 g) haloumi cheese, cut into $\frac{1}{4}$-inch (0.5 cm) slices, then quartered

4 sprigs fresh mint, stemmed and leaves torn or roughly chopped

1. Arrange watermelon on a serving plate and drizzle with vinegar.

2. Heat a nonstick skillet over medium-high heat. Add haloumi and cook until golden and soft, about 2 to 3 minutes per side.

3. Immediately place hot haloumi on top of watermelon and sprinkle with mint.

TIPS

The shapes just serve as guidance for what looks nice; as long as the pieces are not too dissimilar in size, you can't go wrong.

This dish is best served immediately to experience the contrast between the warm haloumi and chilled watermelon; however, it can also be enjoyed at room temperature.

Sheet Pan Greek Salad

This is a delicious way to turn a Greek salad into dinner, with soft roasted vegetables and melting feta. Enjoy it as a healthy meal for two or serve it alongside Pork Souvlaki (page 127) and pita bread.

Makes 2 servings

Preheat oven to 400°F (200°C)

Baking sheet, lined with parchment paper

- 1 can (14 oz/398 g) chickpeas, drained and rinsed
- 1 red bell pepper, sliced into strips
- 1 red onion, sliced
- ¼ cup (60 mL) pitted kalamata olives
- 3 oz (90 g) cherry tomatoes, halved
- 3 oz (90 g) feta cheese, crumbled
- 1 tbsp dried oregano
- 2 tbsp (30 mL) olive oil
- 1 small cucumber, shaved or sliced

1. In a large bowl, combine chickpeas, red pepper, onion, olives, tomatoes, feta and oregano. Drizzle with olive oil and toss to coat evenly.
2. Spread mixture on prepared baking sheet. Bake for 20 minutes, or until feta is golden and vegetables are soft.
3. Transfer baked mixture to a serving dish and top with cucumber. Serve warm or at room temperature.

Tips

Add a squeeze of fresh lemon juice before serving for an extra burst of flavor.

Pair with warmed pita bread or a side of tzatziki for a more filling meal.

Tuna Steaks with Oregano Dressing

This simple warm dressing is all that's needed with fresh grilled fish. By warming the oregano gently in oil before serving, the flavor infuses wonderfully. Serve this main with wilted spinach and boiled new potatoes or accompanied by our Sheet Pan Greek Salad (page 123).

Makes 2 servings

Grill pan

2 yellowfin tuna steaks (6 to 8 oz/175 to 250 g each)

¼ tsp salt

¼ tsp freshly ground black pepper

Extra virgin olive oil

¼ cup (60 mL) lemon juice

2 tbsp (30 mL) finely chopped fresh oregano leaves

1. Pat tuna dry and season both sides with salt and pepper.
2. In a small saucepan over low heat, combine ¼ cup (60 mL) oil, lemon juice and oregano. Warm for 5 minutes, then turn off heat while cooking tuna.
3. Heat 1 tbsp oil in a grill pan or skillet over medium-high heat. Sear steaks for 2 to 3 minutes per side, or until cooked to your desired doneness (see tip).
4. Place tuna on serving plates and drizzle with warm oregano dressing.

TIPS

For maximum freshness, it's worth purchasing the tuna from the fishmonger on the day you want to serve this dish.

Tuna is best served rare to medium-rare for optimal flavor and texture. Medium-rare tuna will be just warm inside, with seared edges. Rare tuna will be cool inside.

Use the warm dressing to coat lima beans for a delicious side dish.

Chicken Tinga with Oregano

This recipe calls for Mexican oregano, which has a slightly more pungent aroma than regular oregano, although either will work. This tinga is perfect as a filling for tacos and wraps or for topping tostadas and rice bowls.

Makes 6 servings

Dutch oven with lid

2 tbsp (30 mL) olive oil

1 onion, thinly sliced

3 cloves garlic, minced

1 tbsp dried Mexican oregano

1 tsp ground cumin

2 canned chipotle peppers with adobo sauce, minced (see tip)

1 can (26 oz/700 mL) diced tomatoes

¾ cup (175 mL) ready-to-use chicken broth

1 tsp apple cider vinegar

2 lbs (1 kg) boneless skinless chicken thighs

Salt and freshly ground black pepper

1. In a Dutch oven, heat oil over medium heat. Add onion and sauté for 5 minutes or until softened. Add garlic, oregano and cumin and cook until fragrant, about 1 minute.

2. Add chipotle peppers, diced tomatoes, broth and vinegar to the Dutch oven. Bring sauce to a boil.

3. Add chicken and turn heat to low. Cover with a lid and cook for 30 minutes.

4. When chicken juices run clear and it shreds easily, remove chicken from sauce and shred with two forks.

5. Increase heat and reduce sauce until thickened, about 5 minutes.

6. Return chicken to Dutch oven, stir to coat in sauce and season to taste with salt and pepper before serving.

TIPS

Chipotle peppers in adobo sauce are widely available, usually in cans, and are softened in a spicy-tangy sauce, making them very convenient to use.

Leftovers can be frozen in an airtight container for up to 3 months.

Pork Souvlaki

This flavorful, tender pork souvlaki is marinated in a simple Mediterranean blend packed with oregano. If you're able to cook it on a barbecue or in a griddle pan, the results are worth it.

Makes 6 servings

12 wooden skewers, soaked in cold water for at least 1 hour

SOUVLAKI

2 tbsp (30 mL) lemon juice

2 tbsp (30 mL) olive oil

1 tbsp dried oregano

1 tsp mild paprika

1 tsp garlic powder

1 tsp salt

1½ lbs (750 g) pork tenderloin, cut into 1-inch (2.5 cm) cubes

Pita bread or wraps, to serve

TZATZIKI

1 cup (250 mL) Greek yogurt

1 (4 oz/125 g) cucumber, skin on, grated and pat dry with a paper towel

½ tsp salt

Freshly ground black pepper

1. *Souvlaki:* In a large bowl, combine lemon juice, oil, oregano, paprika, garlic powder and salt. Add pork and toss to coat thoroughly. Cover and marinate in the refrigerator for 1 to 24 hours.
2. Thread marinated pork evenly onto skewers, making sure the pieces are close together.
3. Heat a barbecue or grill pan over medium-high heat. Cook pork skewers, turning occasionally, until pork is lightly charred and cooked through, with just a hint of pink, about 8 to 10 minutes.
4. *Tzatziki:* In a small bowl, stir together yogurt, cucumber and salt, and season with pepper, to taste.
5. Serve souvlaki with tzatziki and warmed pita bread.

TIPS

For authentic Greek gyros-style, wrap pita around oven-baked French fries with pork and tzatziki.

Replace pork with chicken breast and cook in the same way (chicken is done when there is no pink inside).

Seafood Paella

Paella is traditionally made in a paella pan, which is a shallow pan with a wide surface area, but a large, deep skillet will work just fine. This classic dish combines vibrant vegetables and fresh seafood with a Spanish spice staple, paprika. This one-pan meal can be served on its own or with a green salad.

Makes 6 servings

CAUTION!
Mussel shells will open when cooked; discard any that do not open, as they are not safe to eat.

- 4 cups (1 L) ready-to-use chicken broth
- 1 tsp smoked paprika
- 1 tsp sweet paprika
- 1 pinch saffron threads
- $\frac{1}{3}$ cup (75 mL) olive oil
- 3 cloves garlic, crushed
- 1 red bell pepper, sliced into strips
- 1$\frac{1}{2}$ cups (375 mL) paella rice (see tip)
- 1 large tomato, diced
- 1 cup (250 mL) shelled peas
- 8 baby octopuses, cleaned
- 12 prawns, peeled and deveined
- 6 mussels, scrubbed and debearded
- Salt and freshly ground black pepper
- 1 lemon, cut into wedges

1. Heat broth in a medium saucepan over medium heat. Add smoked paprika, sweet paprika and saffron to hot broth, stir and set aside.
2. Heat oil in a large, deep skillet over medium heat, then add garlic and red pepper and pan-fry until softened, about 3 minutes.
3. Stir in rice, ensuring it is well combined.
4. Pour prepared broth into skillet. Stir to combine, then cover lightly with a lid or foil and cook over medium-low heat until nearly all the broth is absorbed and rice is nearly cooked, about 20 to 25 minutes.
5. Arrange tomatoes, peas, octopus, prawns and mussels evenly on top of rice. Cover again and cook until mussels open and the prawns are cooked through (see note of caution, at left). Season to taste with salt and pepper.
6. Remove from heat and serve from the skillet at the table, with lemon wedges.

TIP

Paella rice is a short-grain rice like Arborio, which can also be used in this recipe.

VARIATION

Replace seafood with 10 to 14 oz (300 to 400 g) chicken breasts (about 2), cut into 1-inch (2.5 cm) pieces.

Smoky Brunch Eggs with Peppers and Paprika

This popular brunch dish (shakshuka) is found all around the Middle East, combining spiced peppers, spices, tomatoes and eggs, cooked together in one pan. Serve with warm pita bread or toast drizzled in olive oil.

Makes 4 servings

- 1 tbsp olive oil
- 7 red and yellow bell peppers, seeded and sliced lengthways into strips
- 1 large red onion, sliced
- 4 cloves garlic, crushed
- 1½ tsp smoked paprika
- ½ tsp ground cumin
- ½ tsp urfa biber chile flakes (or other mild chile flakes)
- 1 can (28 oz/796 mL) diced tomatoes
- 3 cups (750 mL) loosely packed baby spinach
- Salt, to taste
- 4 to 8 eggs (depending on whether you allow 1 or 2 eggs per person)

1. Heat olive oil in a large, deep skillet over low heat. Add bell peppers, onion and garlic. Stir and cook mixture until starting to soften, about 5 minutes.

2. Sprinkle in smoked paprika, ground cumin and urfa biber chile flakes. Stir well to coat vegetables.

3. Pour in tomatoes and stir to combine. Cover the skillet with a lid and cook over low heat, stirring occasionally, until vegetables are tender, about 15 to 20 minutes.

4. Stir in baby spinach and cook until wilted. Season with salt to taste.

5. Using the back of a spoon, make small indents in the tomatoes mixture for the eggs. Crack eggs directly into the indents. Cover the skillet with the lid and cook over low heat until eggs are cooked, about 5 to 7 minutes, or to your desired doneness. Serve immediately.

VARIATION

Meat lovers can add sliced chorizo to the pan with the vegetables in step 1.

Beef Stroganoff

Beef stroganoff originated in Russia, but has been a Western favorite since the 1950s, with many variations. The traditional recipe features tender beef, earthy mushrooms and a rich, creamy paprika sauce. Serve it with egg noodles, mashed potatoes or rice.

Makes 4 servings

- 1 tbsp all-purpose flour
- ½ tsp salt
- ½ tsp freshly ground black pepper
- 1 lb (500 g) sirloin steak, cut into strips
- 1 tbsp butter
- 1 onion, halved and thinly sliced
- 1 clove garlic, minced
- 3½ oz (105 g) cremini (Swiss brown) mushrooms, sliced
- 1 tbsp vegetable oil
- 2 tsp sweet paprika
- ½ tsp smoked paprika
- 1 cup (250 mL) ready-to-use beef broth
- 2 tsp tomato paste
- ¼ cup (60 mL) sour cream
- 2 tsp Dijon mustard
- 2 tbsp (30 mL) finely chopped fresh parsley

1. In a medium bowl, combine the flour, salt and pepper. Add steak and toss in the mixture until completely coated.

2. Heat butter in a large skillet over medium heat. Add onion and cook until softened, about 2 to 3 minutes. Add garlic and mushrooms, and cook, stirring occasionally, until mushrooms are tender, about 3 minutes. Transfer mushrooms mixture to a plate.

3. Heat oil in the same skillet over medium-high heat and add beef. Cook, stirring occasionally, until browned on all sides, about 3 minutes.

4. Return onion and mushroom mixture to skillet and add sweet paprika and smoked paprika, stirring to combine.

5. Add broth and tomato paste, stirring gently; bring to a simmer (do not boil) and cook for 5 minutes.

6. Lower heat and stir in sour cream and mustard until smooth. Cook for 5 minutes to thicken.

7. Serve hot, with parsley sprinkled on top.

TIP

Sirloin is a lean cut of meat that requires minimal cooking time; it can be served while still pink inside.

Spicy Wings

These wings are great for game day or for feeding a crowd of hungry teens. This recipe's mouthwatering combination of spices combined with a fail-safe method of cooking means these wings will disappear in moments.

Makes 8 to 10 servings

2 baking sheets, lined with parchment paper

3 lbs (1.5 kg) chicken wings, tips removed (see tip)

$\frac{1}{4}$ cup (60 mL) olive oil

2 tbsp (30 mL) hot paprika

2 tsp salt

1 tsp ground cumin

1 tsp ground cinnamon

1 tsp ground ginger

1 tsp garlic powder

1 tsp ground mild chili

$\frac{1}{2}$ tsp ground allspice

1. In a large bowl, toss wings in oil, paprika, salt, cumin, cinnamon, ginger, garlic powder, ground chili and allspice, ensuring they are completely covered (using your hands is best).
2. Cover and refrigerate for at least 1 hour (or overnight).
3. Heat oven to 325°F (160°C), and arrange wings on prepared baking sheets in a single layer. When oven is hot, cook wings for 60 minutes, turning once halfway through cooking time.
4. Increase oven temperature to 425°F (220°C) and cook wings for 20 minutes, until the skin is crispy.
5. Let cool slightly before serving.

TIPS

The chicken wing tips are thin and bony, so removing them prevents burning and leaves the meatier parts to cook evenly.

Serve the wings with cooling blue cheese or ranch dressing for dipping.

Tomato and Rosemary Tart

This four-ingredient tart makes a perfect light lunch served in the garden on a summer's day. Pair it with Watermelon, Haloumi and Mint Salad (page 120) and Virgin Mojitos (page 118).

Makes 6 servings

Preheat oven to 350°F (180°C)

Baking sheet, lined with parchment paper

1 sheet puff pastry (12 by 10 inches/30 by 25 cm)

3½ oz (105 g) Gruyère cheese, grated

3 large ripe red tomatoes, sliced

2 tbsp (30 mL) finely chopped fresh rosemary

1. Transfer puff pastry sheet to prepared baking sheet. Cut a ½-inch (1 cm) strip from each pastry sheet edge. Create a raised border by placing each strip on an edge of the larger pastry sheet, trimming any excess pastry as needed.
2. Sprinkle half the cheese and half the rosemary on base of tart, then arrange tomatoes on top.
3. Sprinkle remaining cheese and remaining rosemary on top of tomatoes.
4. Bake in preheated oven for 20 minutes or until pastry is golden and crisp. Cut into squares and serve.

TIPS

The assembled tart can be covered and refrigerated for up to 2 hours before baking.

Use a variety of colored heirloom tomatoes, if available.

VARIATION

Spread 2 tbsp (30 mL) black olive tapenade on the pastry base at the start of step 2.

Roast Rosemary Lamb Shoulder

In this recipe, lamb shoulder benefits from being marinated overnight with rosemary, garlic and lemon, then slow-roasted until the meat is fall-apart tender. Serve with crisp oven-roasted potatoes and steamed vegetables for the ultimate Sunday night dinner or for any special occasion.

Makes 6 to 8 servings

Deep roasting pan

4$\frac{1}{2}$ lbs (2.25 kg) lamb shoulder
8 cloves garlic
8 sprigs fresh rosemary
3 shallots, roughly chopped
1 lemon, sliced
3 tbsp (45 mL) olive oil
1 tsp salt
2 cups (500 mL) water or broth

1. In a large bowl, stir together lamb, garlic, rosemary, shallots, lemon, oil and salt. Make sure lamb is well-coated with the marinade. Cover bowl with plastic wrap and refrigerate overnight.

2. Preheat oven to 250°F (120°C). Spread marinade evenly around bottom of deep roasting pan and place lamb in it. Pour 2 cups (500 mL) water into pan, ensuring it surrounds the lamb. Cover pan tightly with aluminum foil.

3. Roast for 3 hours or until the meat is tender and pulls away easily from the bone. Increase oven temperature to 375°F (190°C) and cook, uncovered, for 20 minutes.

4. Transfer lamb to a serving platter. Strain the juices from the pan to serve as a sauce, if desired.

TIP

Leftover lamb is wonderful served in pita bread with hummus.

Classic Cassoulet

This rustic, French-inspired dish combines pork sausages and a hearty mix of beans, simmered in a rich, spiced tomato and red wine sauce. This satisfying cassoulet is perfect for cooler weather. It can be served simply with crusty bread.

Makes 4 servings

Dutch oven

2 tsp olive oil

1 red onion, finely chopped

2 cloves garlic, minced

1 red bell pepper, chopped

6 pork sausages, sliced into $\frac{1}{2}$-inch (1 cm) pieces (see tip)

2 anchovy fillets, chopped

1 can (14 oz/398 mL) crushed tomatoes

1 cup (250 mL) lima beans, drained and rinsed

1 cup (250 mL) black-eyed peas, drained and rinsed

1 cup (250 mL) dry red wine

1$\frac{1}{2}$ tbsp dried rosemary

1 tsp dried thyme

1 tsp paprika

Sea salt and freshly ground black pepper

1. In Dutch oven, heat olive oil over medium heat. Add red onion and sauté until translucent, about 5 minutes. Stir in garlic and red pepper; cook until softened, about 2 minutes.

2. Add sausages and cook, stirring occasionally, until browned on both sides, about 6 minutes.

3. Add anchovies, tomatoes, lima beans, black-eyed peas, wine, rosemary, thyme and paprika. Stir well to combine.

4. Reduce heat to low and simmer, stirring occasionally, until sauce has thickened and sausage is tender, about 30 minutes.

5. Season to taste with salt and pepper. Ladle cassoulet into bowls and serve right away.

TIPS

Use high-quality pork sausages (from a farmers' market or butcher, without unnecessary fillers) for the best flavor. A garlic or herbed variety such as Toulouse works particularly well.

This cassoulet can be made up to 2 days in advance and stored in the refrigerator, covered. Reheat gently over low heat, adding a splash of water or wine if the sauce has thickened too much.

VARIATION

Add meat from 2 confit duck legs, shredded, in step 3 for a richer cassoulet.

Rosemary Vegetable Skewers

This is a fun and impressive side dish to serve at a barbecue. This aromatic dish uses fresh rosemary sprigs as both seasoning and skewers, adding a subtle herbal flavor to the grilled haloumi and vegetables. You can experiment with different vegetables, and even meat.

Makes 8 skewers

8 sprigs fresh rosemary, 6 to 8 inches (15 to 20 cm)

8 oz (250 g) haloumi cheese, cut into ½-inch (1 cm) cubes

1 red bell pepper, cut into ½-inch (1 cm) pieces

1 zucchini, cut into ½-inch (1 cm) cubes

1 tbsp olive oil

2 tsp lemon zest

1 tsp garlic powder

1. Strip leaves from bottom three-quarters of each rosemary sprig, leaving a cluster of leaves at the top. This creates a bare "stick" for threading ingredients.
2. Thread haloumi, red pepper and zucchini evenly onto each rosemary skewer, alternating ingredients for some nice color variation.
3. In a small bowl, combine oil, lemon zest and garlic powder. Brush mixture over the assembled skewers, coating evenly.
4. Heat a barbecue or griddle pan over medium-high heat. Cook skewers, turning occasionally, for 4 to 6 total minutes. The vegetables should be tender, and the haloumi should be soft with light grill marks.
5. Transfer skewers to a serving plate and enjoy them warm.

TIPS

To prevent rosemary skewers from burning, soak the sprigs in water for 30 minutes before assembling. This is more important if adding meat to the recipe, because of the longer cooking time.

Assemble the skewers through step 2 up to 2 days ahead and store in an airtight container in the refrigerator.

VARIATION

Use cremini (Swiss brown) mushrooms and green bell peppers for a wintertime twist.

Quick Chicken Pot Pie

This creamy chicken and thyme pie is perfect for a quick family meal served with a simple green salad or steamed broccoli. Even better — it can be prepared ahead and frozen! This recipe can make one large pie or four individual pies.

Makes 4 servings

Preheat oven to 400°F (200°C)

8-inch (20 cm) pie plate

- 1 tbsp olive oil
- 2 leeks, sliced
- 1 large clove garlic, crushed
- 10 oz (300 g) baby spinach
- 14 oz (400 g) chicken breasts, cut into 1-inch (2.5 cm) cubes
- $\frac{1}{4}$ tsp salt
- $\frac{1}{4}$ tsp freshly ground black pepper
- $\frac{3}{4}$ cup (175 mL) light crème fraîche
- 1 tbsp whole-grain mustard
- 2 tsp fresh thyme leaves
- 1 sheet (12 by 10 inches/30 by 25 cm) ready-rolled puff pastry
- 1 large egg yolk, beaten

1. In a large skillet, heat oil over medium heat. Sauté leeks and garlic until soft, about 3 minutes. Transfer to a large bowl.
2. Add spinach to the same skillet and stir, still over medium heat, until wilted. Transfer spinach to a sieve and press to drain excess moisture; add spinach to bowl with leeks.
3. Season chicken with salt and pepper. Add to skillet and cook, turning occasionally, for 5 to 6 minutes, until browned on all sides. Chicken does not need to be cooked through, as it will finish cooking in the oven. Add chicken to the bowl with leeks and spinach.
4. Add crème fraîche, mustard and thyme to the same bowl and stir, ensuring everything is well combined.
5. Spoon filling into pie plate. Place puff pastry over the top, trimming any excess. Brush pastry with beaten egg.
6. Place pie in preheated oven and bake for 25 minutes, or until the pastry has risen and looks golden.

TIP

If preparing pie ahead of time, let filling cool completely before placing pastry on top. This prevents steam from softening the pastry, ensuring a flaky texture when baked.

VARIATION

For a curry chicken pie, add 1 tbsp mild curry powder to crème fraîche instead of mustard and thyme in step 4.

Roasted Honey and Thyme Carrots

These tender, golden roasted carrots are infused with hints of warming ginger, sweet honey and fresh, herbaceous thyme, making them a perfect side dish for a Thanksgiving or Christmas meal.

Makes 4 servings

Preheat oven to 400°F (200°C)

Baking sheet, lined with parchment

1 lb (500 g) unpeeled carrots, scrubbed, cut into even 4-inch (10 cm) pieces, then cut in half lengthways

1 tbsp butter

1½ tsp runny honey

1 tbsp fresh thyme leaves

¼ tsp ground ginger

Salt and freshly ground black pepper

1. In a large pot of boiling water, cook carrots, until partially tender, about 10 minutes. Drain and return them to the hot pot.

2. Add butter, honey, thyme and ginger to carrots. Season to taste with salt and pepper. Stir well to coat evenly.

3. Transfer carrots to prepared baking sheet, spreading them out evenly. Roast in preheated oven for 30 to 40 minutes, or until tender and golden, turning halfway through.

TIP

These roasted carrots can be cut into smaller pieces and added to warm salads.

Easy Mushroom and Thyme Pâté

This pâté is a great vegetarian appetizer, and individual portions in small ramekins are perfect for dinner parties (see tip). The flavor of earthy thyme with mushrooms works together extremely well. Serve this tasty pâté with crackers or crostini.

Makes 2 cups (500 mL)

Food processor (or blender)

2 tbsp (30 mL) butter
1 tbsp olive oil
1 shallot, chopped
1 clove garlic, crushed
12 oz (375 g) mixed wild mushrooms, roughly chopped
2 tsp dried thyme
$\frac{1}{2}$ tsp salt
$\frac{1}{2}$ tsp freshly ground black pepper
$\frac{1}{2}$ cup (125 mL) crème fraîche

1. In a large skillet, heat butter and oil over medium heat. Once butter has melted, add shallot and garlic and cook, stirring often, until softened but not browned, about 3 to 4 minutes.
2. Add mushrooms and thyme, then reduce heat to low.
3. Cook, stirring occasionally, until all liquid has evaporated and mushrooms are tender, about 20 minutes. Season to taste with salt and pepper.
4. Blitz mushroom mixture in food processor or blender until smooth. Stir crème fraîche into pâté mixture until well combined. Press into a serving dish, cover with plastic wrap and refrigerate for at least 1 hour before serving. The pâté should be firm but still spreadable.

TIPS

If you don't have a food processor or blender, finely chop mushrooms, which will give the pâté a more rustic texture.

Divide pâté evenly into small ramekins for individual servings. This will make approximately six $\frac{1}{2}$-cup (125 mL) portions.

Squash Salad with Blue Cheese and Bacon

This delicious, fall-inspired salad is ideal as a side dish or light main course. The sweetness of the roasted squash with fragrant thyme pairs wonderfully with crispy bacon, tangy blue cheese and the crunch of toasted pine nuts.

Makes 4 servings or 6 as a side dish

Preheat oven to 350°F (180°C)

Baking sheet, lined with parchment paper

1 (1 lb/500 g) squash, peeled and cut into 1-inch (2.5 cm) cubes

2 tbsp (30 mL) olive oil, divided

2 tbsp (30 mL) dried thyme leaves

1 tsp salt

8 slices bacon, diced

2 cups (500 mL) baby spinach

2 tsp apple cider vinegar

2 tbsp (30 mL) pine nuts, toasted (see tip)

3½ oz (105 g) blue cheese (such as Roquefort)

1. In large bowl, toss squash with 1 tbsp oil, thyme and salt. Spread on prepared baking sheet and roast for 40 minutes, turning once, until tender and golden brown.

2. While squash roasts, cook bacon in a large skillet over medium heat until crispy. Drain on a paper towel.

3. In medium bowl, toss spinach in vinegar and remaining oil, and arrange on a serving plate.

4. Top with squash, bacon and pine nuts, then crumble blue cheese over the top, and serve.

TIP

To toast pine nuts, cook them in a dry skillet over medium heat, shaking skillet lightly for about 2 minutes, until lightly golden. Remove from heat as soon as they start to color.

VARIATION

Add 8 oz (250 g) Brussels sprouts, trimmed, to squash when baking in step 1 for a festive twist.

Coconut Fish Curry

This fragrant curry combines a creamy coconut milk base with a homemade spice paste, tender white fish and crisp sugar snap peas. Enjoy it with steamed rice or rice noodles for a delicious, immunity-boosting meal.

Makes 4 servings

Food processor or mortar and pestle

- 2 tbsp (30 mL) vegetable or coconut oil
- 2 cloves garlic, roughly chopped
- 2 stems fresh cilantro
- ½ shallot or small yellow onion, roughly chopped
- ½ long red chile (see tip)
- 1 tbsp roughly chopped fresh gingerroot
- 2 tsp ground turmeric
- 1 tsp ground coriander seed
- ½ tsp ground cumin
- ½ tsp salt
- Pinch ground cardamom
- 1 can (14 oz/400 mL) coconut milk
- 1 lb (500 g) skinless firm white fish (e.g., cod), cut into 1-inch (2.5 cm) pieces
- 1 cup (250 mL) sugar snap peas or snow peas, cut in half
- 3 tbsp (45 mL) lime juice
- Cilantro leaves, for garnish

1. In small bowl of food processor, or using a mortar and pestle, combine oil, garlic, cilantro stems, shallot, chile, ginger, turmeric, coriander seed, cumin, salt and cardamom. Blitz or pound until a rough paste forms.
2. Heat a large skillet or wok over medium heat. Add spice paste and sauté, stirring frequently, until fragrant, 1 to 2 minutes.
3. Stir in coconut milk and bring to a gentle simmer for 2 to 3 minutes. Add fish and simmer gently for 5 minutes.
4. Add sugar snap peas and lime juice; cook until fish is opaque and flakes easily when tested with a fork and peas are just tender, about 2 to 3 minutes.
5. Serve garnished with fresh cilantro leaves.

TIPS

If you prefer a milder chile heat, remove seeds before using.

Spice paste can be frozen in a small airtight container for up to 6 months. Freeze in ice cube trays, transfer to a sealable plastic bag and store in the freezer for single-serve portions.

Cauliflower Popcorn

Forget traditional popcorn; these golden, spiced cauliflower bites are a healthy snack or side packed with color and flavor. They are also a novel addition to salads and grain bowls.

Makes 4 servings

Preheat oven to 350°F (180°C)

Baking sheet, lined with parchment

¼ cup (60 mL) plain Greek yogurt
½ tsp salt
½ tsp ground turmeric
¼ tsp ground cumin
¼ tsp smoked paprika
1 lb (500 g) cauliflower florets, cut into bite-size pieces (about 1 inch/2.5 cm)
Additional salt

1. In a large bowl, combine yogurt, salt, turmeric, cumin and paprika to form a wet marinade.
2. Add cauliflower to the bowl and toss until evenly coated with marinade (this is easiest done by hand).
3. Spread coated cauliflower in a single layer on prepared baking sheet.
4. Bake in preheated oven for 45 minutes, turning halfway through, until the cauliflower is golden and slightly crisp.
5. Sprinkle with additional salt to taste and serve warm.

Variation

Add 1 cup (250 mL) chickpeas, drained, rinsed and dried, to bowl with cauliflower in step 2.

Singapore Noodles

This is classic Asian street food, originating in China (not Singapore!). These noodles have a vibrant yellow color due to the turmeric and additional spices. This dish has many variations, often including chicken and Asian sausage.

Makes 4 servings

- 8 oz (250 g) dried rice vermicelli noodles
- 2 tbsp (30 mL) vegetable oil, divided
- 2 large eggs, lightly beaten
- 1 small onion, thinly sliced
- 2 cloves garlic, minced
- 1 red bell pepper, thinly sliced
- 1 medium carrot, julienned
- ½ cup (125 mL) snow peas, sliced in half diagonally
- 1 tsp ground coriander seed
- 1 tsp ground turmeric
- ½ tsp ground cumin
- ½ tsp freshly ground black pepper
- ½ tsp hot pepper flakes or cayenne
- 2 tbsp (30 mL) soy sauce
- 1 tbsp oyster sauce
- 1 tbsp sesame oil
- 1 tbsp rice wine vinegar
- 1 tsp sugar
- 1 cup (250 mL) bean sprouts, to serve

1. Soak noodles in warm water (not boiling) until softened but still firm to the bite, about 10 minutes. Drain.

2. Heat 1 tbsp vegetable oil in a large skillet or wok over medium heat. Pour in beaten eggs and cook, stirring gently, to create soft scrambled eggs. Transfer to a chopping board; roughly chop into bite-size pieces.

3. Add remaining vegetable oil to skillet. Stir-fry onion and garlic for 1 minute. Add red pepper, carrot and snow peas, and stir-fry until vegetables are slightly tender but still crisp, about 2 minutes.

4. Add coriander seed, turmeric, cumin, black pepper and hot pepper flakes to skillet, stirring to coat vegetables, for 1 minute. Add drained noodles to skillet and toss to combine.

5. In a small bowl, whisk together soy sauce, oyster sauce, sesame oil, vinegar and sugar. Pour sauce over noodle mixture and toss well to coat evenly. Return scrambled eggs to skillet and toss gently to incorporate.

6. Serve immediately, with bean sprouts sprinkled on top.

VARIATION

For an even more substantial dish, include cooked shrimp, chicken or tofu. Stir-fry it separately before step 3 and add it back with the eggs in step 5.

Turmeric Chai Chia Pudding

This vegan chia pudding takes inspiration from turmeric chai, combining warm spices with the earthy richness of this exotic spice. This nutritious, satisfying breakfast, snack or dessert can be prepared ahead of time for convenience. Serve this chia pudding chilled with toppings like sliced bananas, toasted coconut flakes or chopped almonds, or a drizzle of honey.

Makes 2 servings

1 cup (250 mL) non-dairy milk, such as almond, soy or oat
½ tsp ground cinnamon
¼ tsp ground turmeric
¼ tsp ground cardamom
⅛ tsp ground ginger
Pinch freshly ground black pepper
1 tsp pure maple syrup (adjust to taste)
¼ cup (60 mL) chia seeds
½ tsp vanilla extract

1. In a small saucepan, combine milk, cinnamon, turmeric, cardamom, ginger, pepper and maple syrup. Heat over medium-low heat, stirring frequently, until just warm and the spices are fully dissolved, about 5 minutes. Do not boil.

2. Remove from heat and let mixture cool slightly.

3. In a medium bowl, combine turmeric chai milk mixture, chia seeds and vanilla. Stir well to combine. Let sit for 5 minutes, then stir again to prevent clumping. Keep in bowl or spoon into two small serving bowls.

4. Cover and refrigerate for at least 2 hours, or overnight, until chia seeds have absorbed liquid and the pudding is thick and creamy.

TIPS

Double the batch for easy meal prep throughout the week. Chia pudding can be stored in a container in the fridge for up to 5 days.

Spoon pudding into crystal glasses and top with whipped coconut cream and a dusting of cinnamon for a healthy end to an evening meal.

Enjoy sharing with family and friends.

Acknowledgments

For both of us, embarking on writing a beginner's book on how to add flavor with herbs and spices was a surprisingly daunting task, made all the more enjoyable as a father and daughter team! While our award-winning books on herbs and spices contained extensive detail, from our combined positions of over 50 years in the spice industry, and experience as a qualified chef and recipe developer, the objective of this book was to make an amazing world of flavor accessible to everyone.

While *The Spice and Herb Bible*'s 800 pages of information may be the next step on a spice journey, this beautifully crafted edition has distilled so much useful knowledge with the support of many people who have been involved since its inception.

Foremost is the constant and unwavering support of publisher Bob Dees of Robert Rose Inc. A publisher who has supported us for over 20 years and maintained faith in our ability to deliver high quality, accurate and engaging work. This book has achieved great clarity of communication through the editorial work by Amy Treadwell and designer Kevin Cockburn of PageWave Graphics.

Our accumulation of knowledge through our obsession with spices, would not have been possible if it were not for the generous sharing of information by so many people in the spice industry too numerous to mention here. These included traders, farmers and their families and the late Dr. P.S. Sreekanthan Thampi from the Spices Board in India.

Finally, we give special gratitude to Rosemary, mother and beloved grandmother who was a true pioneer in cookbook writing with herbs and spices. Heartfelt thanks also go to our tireless taste-testing team—Keith, Maisie, and Lochy—whose dinners, more often than not, involved new recipes in need of honest feedback.

The support, wise counsel and initial editorial guidance provided by wife and mother Elizabeth, made the creation of *How to Add Flavor* a wonderful family experience..

— Ian Hemphill and Kate McIntosh

Index

Q

R

S

Library and Archives Canada Cataloguing in Publication

Title: How to add flavor : an introduction to spices & herbs / Ian Hemphill & Kate McIntosh.
Names: Hemphill, Ian, 1949- author | McIntosh, Kate, author
Description: Includes index.
Identifiers: Canadiana 20250159414 | ISBN 9780778807346 (softcover)
Subjects: LCSH: Spices. | LCSH: Herbs. | LCSH: Cooking (Spices) | LCSH: Cooking (Herbs) | LCGFT: Cookbooks.
Classification: LCC TX406 .H42 2025 | DDC 641.6/383—dc23